GLOBAL BOHEMIAN

GLOBAL BOHEMIAN

HOW TO SATISFY YOUR WANDERLUST AT HOME

Fifi O'Neill

Photography by Mark Lohman

CICO BOOKS
LONDON NEW YORK

Published in 2019 by CICO Books
An imprint of Ryland Peters & Small Ltd
20–21 Jockey's Fields   341 E 116th St
London WC1R 4BW   New York, NY 10029

www.rylandpeters.com

10 9 8 7 6 5 4 3

Text © Fifi O'Neill 2019
Design and photography © CICO Books 2019

A CIP catalog record for this book is available from the Library
of Congress and the British Library.

ISBN: 978-1-78249-718-9

Printed in China

Editor: Gillian Haslam
Designer: Louise Leffler
Photographer: Mark Lohman

In-house editor: Anna Galkina
Art director: Sally Powell
Production manager: Gordana Simakovic
Publishing manager: Penny Craig
Publisher: Cindy Richards

CONTENTS

A **DIFFERENT** BEAUTY

Bohemianism has long been associated with artists, musicians, writers, and designers. Affectionately referred to as boho, this layered, vibrant, and organic aesthetic is clearly thriving. If you revel in freedom from conventions and rules, love a home that reflects individuality, spontaneity, a fondness for a fusion of global goods and a distinctive convergence of cultures, bohemian style is pure catnip! From minimal boho touches to full-on Coachella-inspired rooms, relaxed, natural, eclectic, and romantic design elements make the global bohemian home a thing of beauty.

With their blend of styles, the homes featured in the pages of this book boast a uniquely enchanting atmosphere, often reflected in the variety of treasures they showcase—from personal collections to inspired use of color and pattern, these wildly differing living spaces show signs of humanity and the patina of life. Whether you want to transform an understated room by adding whimsical elements or create an exotic oasis in your bedroom, unconventional boho artistry is easy to achieve by incorporating a few basics such as jewel-toned items, metallic touches, alluring prints, and layers of textures, to name but a few. Mismatched pieces from various origins and eras, delicious colors, exquisite textiles, and imaginative displays give spaces an undeniable energy.

This book celebrates the decorating tenets of freethinking, world traveling, and nomadic ideals, and the beauty of self-expression.

ELEMENTS OF GLOBAL STYLE

COLOR

Bohemian-style home décor is for those who want their homes to embrace the carefree, the relaxed, and the unusual, and to be full of life and culture.

Fortunately there are no rules when it comes to boho decorating, and that means you have the freedom to use colors that wouldn't necessarily go together in a conventional way, whether your taste leans to cheerful hues or softer ones. While there is no prescribed color palette for this iconic style, it is often hallmarked by warm hues like deep blue, hot pink, and sunny yellow, which, when combined, bring visual intensity. And for those who like it hot, jewel tones and metallic accents rule.

And somewhere in the middle lies a more muted palette of warm mochas, earthy taupes, and gold-tinged accents, while at the other end of the spectrum we find an even more subdued mood with watercolor hues ranging from cream to blush, and aqua. Regardless of your preference, the backdrop you select provides a dynamic canvas for showcasing your unique style.

ABOVE: From ice blue to deep indigo, vibrant to faded, and everything in between, cool blue hues look great no matter how you style and mix them. Blues and whites are always a good match, especially when you want to feature one or several shades of blue. Soft aqua and its more brilliant cousin turquoise give this small room its cohesiveness and sense of calm. If you prefer not to use strong hues on a large scale, start small, with accessories like pillows, rugs, flowers, books, and lampshades. In this living room the pillows and rug each evoke sea and flora and work together to create a fresh and casual bohemian space.

ABOVE TOP: Yellow, marigold, sunflower, lemon, mustard…few colors have the power to brighten and uplift a space as these. In this living room gold and other similar accents work harmoniously because their intensity is calmed down by the honey tone of the wood floor, and the neutral yet graphic rug. Incorporating a range of the zesty hue through various elements is sure to bring plenty of warmth and cheer to neutral rooms. With their different textures and tones, the sofa, throw, and pillows heighten the comfort quotient. Yellow and its many variations evoke hope, sunshine, and energy.

ABOVE LEFT: Black by itself is striking, but to get real drama and spark, pair it with white. This color combo is both timeless and modern, and works with any style, including boho. The earthy hue of the taupe walls of this bedroom provides the perfect backdrop for a sophisticated black-and-white palette. This classic combination elevates a space and emphasizes elements of the design. It also adds an edge and a contemporary feel, yet remains true to boho style by using fabrics with ethnic patterns to create a sleek and relaxed oasis. Layers and natural elements instill the perfect boho vibe for unwinding.

ABOVE: Layering is at the heart of bohemian decorating. This applies to color as well. Never underestimate the power of paint. Pink might not be the first color that comes to mind when thinking about boho choices, yet its feminine quality brings softness and glamour to a room, especially when paired with metallic and reflective accents. There is no need to paint an entire room when one wall will do the trick. Adding a couple of elements in the same shade family, like the armchair and the glass candleholder featured here, introduces variations on the blush theme and keeps the look from being too sweet.

FURNISHINGS

Boho style is an inspiring mix of old and new, and serious and fanciful, all topped with a big dose of personality. Eclectic is an accurate adjective to define a décor that comprises the heterogeneous elements particular to the global bohemian. There is a fine line, however, between a beautifully diverse design and one that is merely chaotic.

Furniture collected over time and secondhand and vintage items are right at home here. But so are items from around the world, and today global shopping is readily available in bricks-and-mortar stores as well as online. Many vintage and antique finds don't come in pairs, and that's a good thing as mismatched pieces are a plus when it comes to bohemian décor, but every item should be special regardless of its origin. Shop at yard sales, antique markets, and thrift stores to find storied pieces and timeworn and distressed items to create a lived-in, casual interior. For an exotic mood, you can feed your wanderlust for exquisite objects from around the world —from Africa to India, Uzbekistan to Latin America and more with just a click. It has never been easier or more exciting to pack personality and global style into every space in your home. Conformity and uniformity aren't in the boho vocabulary, but individuality is!

OPPOSITE LEFT: An eclectic layering of graphic black-and-white patterns and textures is the hallmark of this casually chic living room. Though diverse in style, the furnishings are united by the palette. The round velvet ottoman balances the angular butterfly-style leather chairs, while rugs with the same color value but different patterns add textural interest and maintain visual unity.

OPPOSITE RIGHT: With its stately mirror paired with a shapely, contemporary bleached-wood side table and twinkling firefly lights, this bedroom corner embodies the boho mix of classic and new, and rustic and refined.

RIGHT: Under a vintage iron-and-crystal chandelier, a lacquered coffee table and a sleek faux-leather loveseat layered with an array of pillows in the same color family but with varied textures set this living room's elegant bohemian vibe.

LEFT: At its very core, globally inspired décor stems from the idea of appreciating world cultures. But instead of focusing on just one culture, mixing accessories from various origins creates a well-rounded, well-traveled look. Accessories should tell your story and highlight the things you love, so family heirlooms, handmade goods, and treasured items from your travels should take center stage. Embracing the natural world is paramount to this style. Whether nestled in woven baskets and colorful pots or hanging in textural macramé, greenery of all sorts brings rooms to life. Add vibrant embellishments such as tassels, pompoms, and fringing and the result is positively ambrosial.

OPPOSITE TOP LEFT: Pairing opposite finishes and styles gives this vignette its unique character and appeal. The frosted vase and the lustrous shells offer a smooth counterpoint to the intricate texture of the Moroccan votive and the delicate filigree design of the lantern. The union of pale and hot pinks with shimmering gold makes the composition dreamy and magical.

OPPOSITE BOTTOM LEFT: Buddha has come to represent peace, tranquility, and understanding, and is embraced in homes and gardens worldwide. Sculpture, like this wooden one, is perhaps the most well-known form of representation for the image of the revered icon. Buddha statues are staples of bohemian décor due to their ability to motivate and inspire people in their quest for attaining inner peace and happiness.

OPPOSITE RIGHT: This patio's relaxed and seductive atmosphere relies on cozy accessories that invite you to linger. Informal and versatile floor pillows provide a form of seating often featured in laid-back spaces, indoor as well as out. Noteworthy goods such as the shibori curtain and pillow introduce tribal notes, while colorful lanterns and a curvaceous candelabrum speak of nomadic adventures.

ACCESSORIES

The global bohemian draws inspiration from many sources. The aesthetic is rooted not only in cultural artifacts but also in pieces that reflect one's personal journey. Weaving together items from a variety of locations for a worldly look is as vital as focusing on gathering unique pieces. It's all about mystery, charm, and the appeal of the unexpected.

Keep in mind that just because the style tends to be offbeat, this doesn't mean it can't be glamorous. Bold accent pieces can bring world-traveler style to any space. Incorporate unconventional elements like floor pillows. Display colorful candle lanterns and include items with metallic gold or silver finishes for a crowning touch to the eclectic décor. Don't forget nature! Vines, succulents, and other houseplants are indispensable for conjuring up the free-spirited, wanderlust feeling of bohemian design.

Once all of your accessories are in place, take a step back to see if everything feels right. If not, continue to make tweaks until you're satisfied with the final results.

ARTISTIC DIPLAYS

Artistic expression is central to boho décor. From paintings to prints, maps, photographs, wall hangings, dream catchers, artifacts, collages, personal mementos, and more, art plays a starring role. These can be smaller investments and an easy way to add a bohemian dimension to any space without incurring major expense.

Aside from grouping items with a similar theme, another way to create an artistic display is to showcase an arrangement that is tied together by color, shape or finish. Thoughtfully combining the dressed-down and frugal facets of bohemia with the sensible and costlier accoutrements of elegant style creates more nuanced and character-filled spaces.

TOP LEFT: Jewelry featuring beads, crosses, hearts, feathers, and tassels is more than just a fashion accessory and is often included as a decorative accent in an artistic composition. But there is more to these gems than meets the eye. Yes, they can be the perfect complement to an outfit, but beautiful and colorful pieces (real or faux, old or new) also make glamorously artistic focal points. Whether you use chunky bracelets as napkin rings, frame vintage necklaces, strategically dangle one-of-a-kind earrings from lampshades or chandeliers, or opt for anatomical sculptures, like this porcelain hand, for an eye-catching accent to style your best baubles, make them part of the décor.

TOP RIGHT: The heart has long been recognized across cultures as being the symbol of love, charity, and compassion. Its universal appeal alone makes it the most appropriate item for homes where mindfulness is the rule. It is also believed to be the center of one's spiritual being and as such is perfect for a soulful boho display, as in this grouping showcasing singular renditions in similar hues but varied finishes.

BOTTOM LEFT: This small but inspiring display curates an enchanting collection of far-flung souvenirs. The gold skull, lantern, cactus, and the textural woven rug, used as a wall hanging, play up the global theme, while the vivid colors and rich patterns in the pots, print, and basket add a rainbow of visual interest.

BOTTOM RIGHT: With its rich history—beginning in East Siberia where nomadic tribes used felt cutouts to embellish the tombs of their deceased—and endless decorative applications and thematic choices, decoupage is a fitting artform for bohemian interiors. While framing postcards from trips can be visually pleasing, composing a collage from copies of favorite photographs of places, people, or events, in either a multitude of colors or in a unifying palette, creates a unique and highly personal artistic display.

FABRIC PATTERNS & TEXTURES

Textiles from various parts of the world, like Africa, Asia, and South America to name a few, reflect a well-traveled vibe and produce distinctive, culturally influenced aesthetics. Much like a good piece of artwork, fabrics can make a room. From rustic burlap to smooth velvet, luxurious silk, nubby wool, hand-woven macramé, worn leather, animal prints, and more, there are plenty of fabulous textile choices to convey a worldly bohemian style and a lush and effortless layered look. With their unique patterns, colorful Navajo tapestries, recycled vintage rugs, patchwork-inspired quilts, and intricate shibori and graphic ikat pillows imply a design collected from faraway bazaars and exotic peddlers.

Pulling off the look is all about layering different fabrics and textures. Tribal prints, patterns, and mixed textures are a hallmark of global bohemian Be sure to mix stripes, paisley, geometric patterns, batik, and tie-dye for a truly unique finish.

TOP LEFT: With their neutral but warm palette and textural characteristics and finishes, a comfy blanket and pillow combine to give this oh-so-boho hanging chair its globally inspired sense of escape, making it an inviting spot to relax or read. The hooked rug's flowery pattern is a nod to nature while also providing another layer of texture and a pop of color.

TOP RIGHT: On this cozy bed, the diverse patterns and finishes go virtually unnoticed thanks to the variety of blues that unify the majority of the textiles in a harmonious yet distinct style.

BOTTOM LEFT: This bedroom embodies the layered look born from a multitude of patterns, textures, and colors. The bedspread's vibrant hues and large-scale floral prints set the exotic tone, while the peachy-pink patterned rug's hues are echoed in the pillows. A curated mix of decorative accessories includes yet more boho-specific elements, like macramé, tassels, and pompoms.

BOTTOM RIGHT: Handcrafted textiles are enjoying considerable popularity in bohemian interiors, and sequined, luxurious Moroccan wedding blankets, or handira, are among the most prized. These works of art are woven from sheep's wool, cotton, and linen, to which hundreds of mirrored sequins are attached by the bride's female relatives. According to Berber customs, the process of hand-weaving, itself, when undertaken mindfully, is thought to endow the textile with baraka, or blessings.

the VINTAGE BOHEMIAN

Joyful, personal, charming, and intriguing, Leslie Nemeth's San Francisco apartment is a pretty good indication of who she is and where she has lived.

Her mother and father are both from Puerto Rico. Her mother's family has roots in Spain, and her father is of African and Hungarian descent. "It's an interesting mix," she notes, "but then most Puerto Ricans tend to have roots in Spain and Africa, as well as tracing their ancestry back to the native Taíno people, indigenous of the Caribbean." As Leslie's father was in the military, she grew up mostly in the US, mainly in Tennessee and Maryland, but also lived for a time in Germany.

As a child, Leslie spent most summers visiting family in Puerto Rico, and when she was 13 her father was stationed there for a year. "I don't know that it consciously influences my decorating, but I do think it's a part of who I am, and that's apparent in my home," she says. "I'm not afraid of color or vibrancy, and Puerto Rico is certainly very colorful and vibrant."

In 2006, Leslie took a road trip down the California coast and fell in love with the landscape and the unique quality of San Francisco. "I decided to make a move, something I'm not particularly intimidated by after moving so much while growing

ABOVE LEFT: A portly, happy Buddha paired with a small metallic pineapple —a traditional feng shui symbol of hospitality, prosperity, and good luck— sets a cheerful and welcoming vignette aptly suited to this upbeat space.

ABOVE RIGHT: This Buddha head came home with Leslie from a trip to China. "The face is so peaceful and serene," she says. "It reminds me that there are so many worlds on this planet and it's a privilege to get to see even a small fraction of it."

OPPOSITE: The red velvet sofa's curvy shape and size bring a sexy and cozy touch to the living room. The small midcentury cabinet's warm wood balances the cooler materials of the coffee and side tables.

PREVIOUS PAGES: The panel of leafy wallpaper pays tribute to Leslie's childhood visits to her family home in Puerto Rico. "It's reminiscent of my great-grandmother's backyard—full of greenery and life and beautiful smells. It makes me happy," she says. The Danish midcentury sideboard was a lucky San Francisco find and provides elegant and much-needed storage. The daybed's low profile not only adds to the bohemian mood but also allows for the room to feel more open. The curtains' subtle pattern ties in with the midcentury pieces while not competing for attention with brighter colors.

LEFT: The cheerful vintage cat pillow, embroidered in blocks of various colors and stitches, is in homage to Leslie's rescued kitty, Turnip.

"There is magic in bohemian style. It's cozy and warm and inviting and exciting all at once. What's not to love?"

OPPOSITE ABOVE: The main room includes the living and the bedroom areas. Leslie chose to tuck the bed off to the side and away from view, creating a little nook-like sleeping space, rather than it becoming a focal point. Her goal was also to avoid blocking the windows. A throw from Afghanistan adds texture and introduces an exotic touch to the neutral bedding. The colorful, free-form crocheted wall hanging on the back of the door was a gift from Leslie's friend Bridget Schwartz, who creates these sculptural pieces using odds and ends of yarn. Next to it hangs a woven rug acquired on a trip to Mexico. The striking cactus print on the adjoining wall is a typical Southern California road-trip scene. "California and Mexico mesh well together," Leslie notes.

ABOVE LEFT: "I've always loved color, and I don't think a room is fully done without art and without texture. I'm drawn to items that remind me of a place I've visited or one I hope to explore, as in the case of the gold, pink, and brown pillow that hails from Turkey. The globe ceiling light reminds me of being in Paris and taking the metro on my way to something wonderful!"

ABOVE RIGHT: Lack of space and love of color dictated the spot for the bicycle. "I think it pairs well with the art hanging there, and I do love pink and green together. It's a pretty bike, so I thought better to display it than have it take up precious storage space!" Leslie says. "The framed print of interlocking hands was one of the first things I purchased after moving in to this space nine years ago—I like the way the woven fingers look like a pattern." The turnip artwork was gifted to Leslie shortly after she adopted her cat, Turnip.

OPPOSITE: When Leslie entertains, the kitchen is the place of choice for friends to gather, play games, and share a meal. Her aim was to create a more intimate and conspiratorial mood, and give the space the feeling of being a separate and entirely different area. The darker wall color, framed vintage pillowcases, low light fixture, graphic rug, macramé table runner, and furnishings establish the warm, inviting mood evocative of a small, clubby lounge.

RIGHT: In spite of the dining area's diminutive size, Leslie managed to set up a bar-like corner by outfitting a vintage filing cabinet repurposed as a cocktail bar with the necessary accoutrements and pairing it with a gold-bamboo mirror with a tiki vibe and a swanky leather chair topped with a cozy faux-fur throw. "It's a great spot to sit and chat, cocktail in hand, while my friends and I take turns cooking dinner in the kitchen. And it's Turnip's favorite chair."

up," she recalls. She found a 600 square-foot studio apartment to rent in a beautiful Art Deco building, "I was immediately charmed by it. The entrance and the façade are really special, and I loved that the building had history and charm. It's definitely not cookie-cutter. And it's rent controlled! That's a huge asset in this city." Though small, the apartment features two main features: ceilings 10 feet high and, in the living room, a full bay of high windows.

Leslie's love affair with decorating goes back to her youth. "My mother was always into interior decorating, and took great care in picking art and furniture. We have different personal styles, but I did inherit from her the conviction that your home should be a reflection of where you've been and where you'd like to go," she says. "Even while in high school I yearned to see Europe, and I absolutely loved vintage French advertisements and deep, beautiful colors. When the movies *Amélie* and *Moulin Rouge* came out in the early 2000s, I was inspired and obsessed with making

A small painting discovered at a garage sale many years ago has become Leslie's little spirit animal—symbolic of travels and adventure.

LEFT: Leslie brought the little bird on a wooden perch back from a trip to Austria. She explains, "The man who makes these uses a method that's hundreds of years old. He captures a bird and then sets it loose in his studio. He studies it and then carves its image out of wood, paints it, and then sets the bird free. It reminds me of the immense natural beauty of Austria and I smile every time I study it." Below the bird hangs a small painting found at a garage sale many years ago, which has become Leslie's spirit animal.

OPPOSITE: The tiles, floor, and cabinets are original to the Art Deco building. Because Leslie is renting the apartment, she is only allowed decorating options. Since the kitchen and eating area share the same space, she continued the deep green wall color to keep consistency. The boho vibe comes in via art. The framed black-and-white portrait was found in a huge vintage warehouse sale. Leslie says, " It simply spoke to me." The red birds inject a vibrant note.

my dorm room cozy and I filled the walls with posters and anything that resembled those movies. I hung tapestries on the wall and I insisted on our room being a gathering place!"

Her lust for travel and desire to see as much of the world as possible also manifested themselves early on. "I think it's because we did move a lot. I was always excited and interested when we went somewhere new— that's just how I'm wired," she explains. "I love that you can easily transform yourself when you travel, but I also think when you're immersed in another culture you get a clearer picture of who you are—travel holds a mirror up to oneself."

France ranks high on Leslie's list of favorite places. "It's the center of Bohemia after all!" she exclaims. "There is magic in bohemian style. It's cozy and warm and inviting and exciting all at once. What's not to love?"

the SOPHISTICATED BOHEMIAN

When two highly creative people team up, magic is sure to follow. And so it was for Kristin Joyce, a visual designer who had worked with high-fashion designers including Diane von Furstenberg, Betsey Johnson, and Karl Lagerfeld, and her husband Don Guy, an award-winning international commercial film director. "We met in New York City and it was love at first sight," Kristin recalls. For the next three years the couple worked in the city, then relocated to San Francisco when Kristin was offered the chance to head the Public Image division of Esprit. Later on, another opportunity brought them to the shores of the Gulf of Mexico on Florida's west coast, a move both Kristin and Don welcomed as they were looking to downsize and indulge their vagabond souls and their love of the beach.

OPPOSITE: Originally a catch-all space located off the kitchen, and in a sad state of disrepair, this once dingy room was transformed into a small but elegant dining area where style meets function. A Noguchi-esque ceiling fixture presides over a Weatherend Estate custom dining table flanked by IKEA slipcovered side chairs. Cherished children's artwork has been framed and given star status. The generous cerulean vessel holds not only a bountiful array of unique shells but also beautiful memories from coastal excursions and a love of beachcombing, swimming, and snorkeling in remote waters off the coasts of Australia, Mexico, and Florida.

ABOVE LEFT: Collected over the years and sourced during numerous trips, ceramics from Italy and Portugal and hand-blown glassware from Norway and Japan inspire colorful and exquisite table settings.

ABOVE RIGHT: The narrow dining room called for few specifically sized and critically placed pieces. A single narrow console and a slender shelf offer the perfect stage for keeping dinner-party items at the ready or simply as a home for beloved books, fresh flowers, or favorite shells, like the unusual collection of razor clam shells gathered on Malahide beach outside of Dublin, Ireland. The gold-framed antique mirror and vintage Italian poster from the 1900s imbue the room with just the right amount of luster, glamour, and drama.

ABOVE LEFT: In the living room, one of two intricately hand-carved, fruitwood chairs—acquired on a trip to Paris, France—sits alongside a modern white console. Floating shelves hold books with subject matters reflecting a love of cultures, global travel, art, and international cookery. In this room the furnishings share a sleek common thread and incorporate art and personal items from travels, resulting in a well-curated interior.

ABOVE RIGHT: The ocelot-print ottoman, converted into a coffee table by the addition of a thick glass top, delivers a dash of whimsy. Gathered around a glass bowl filled with washed-up beach treasures, Kosta Boda glass votives from Sweden shimmer with an icy glow reminiscent of winter lanterns that lit up that country's winter darkness.

ABOVE: Black-and-white and full-color photos are arranged in rows of identical black frames, designed to be easy to update through the years. The driftwood console provides a subtle but strategic separation from the entryway and displays a hand-carved, gold-rubbed wood pineapple lamp, found in a local secondhand store. The substantial Italian carved mirror, discovered on a trip to Carmel, California, captures the natural light spilling from a large window opposite. The neutral palette, enlivened with seafoam and aqua accents, and tactile fabrics, from velvet and linen pillows to a cashmere throw, conveys a crisp, calm feeling. An antique iron daybed from a shop on the Left Bank in Paris, has been converted into a sofa. Weatherend Estate furniture crafted in Maine features two Westport-style chairs.

Don and Kristin have trekked around the globe and their home reflects their interest in many cultures, with a successful mix of design styles creating a rich, organic, modern vibe that works hand-in-hand with a comforting and exotic sensibility. "Decorating is something I can passionately share with Don, who also has an amazing eye for good design." Kristin notes. Her approach to interiors takes its cue partly from the couple's appetite for adventure and respective creativity, but also from Kristin's Scandinavian heritage that reflects her hygge philosophy that she describes as "an appealing quotient for happiness, promoting lifestyle design as a key to emotional well-being."

For Kristin, this emphasis on simple pleasures must include nature and a sense of light, which is accomplished with the home's overall cool palette underscored by a range of coastal whites and watery blues. Her lifelong love of swimming also influences her color sense. "The current choice of brilliant turquoise selected for the living-room accents and the sunroom are reminiscent of an exhilaratingly, beautiful swim in the remote waters off the coast of Greece," she explains.

OPPOSITE: Designed as a respite and sanctuary from a busy life, the bedroom offers a modern sense of calm and contemporary charm. The beautiful and sentimental quilt is overlaid on the simple linens of the streamline platform bed. With a linen silkscreened panel draped over a window, a pair of sculptural white ceramic vases holding fresh garden cuttings, and a luxurious Tibetan sheepskin rug (both from Arhaus), this wonderfully layered, airy, and eclectic space feels invitingly easy and utterly elegant. A limited edition print "Floral Deception," created by friend and international fine-art photographer Alyssia Lazin, and the Possini flowers pendant light provide the finishing touches.

ABOVE LEFT: Maine holds a special place in Kristin's and Don's hearts. The makers at Brooklyn's Haptic Lab Quilts crafted the unique "Penobscot Bay" quilt. It features Swan's Island, Maine where the couple married in a small ceremony on the rugged coast nearly 30 years ago. (Upon purchasing, Kristin sewed a heart in crewel on the exact location.) The one-of-a kind quilt was found in a store in North Haven, Maine during another's wedding celebration many years later. It recollects enchanting and romantic summers spent on the remote island together and, in later years, with their children and close relatives.

ABOVE RIGHT: The Swedish armoire was purchased in New York when the couple first met 35 years ago. It is one of the few keepsakes that has traveled with them from their Manhattan apartment to a first home in Sausalito, a family house in Belvedere, and both of their Florida homes. Kristin honors the beautiful art by friend and painter Pavel Kapic, who works between studios in Tuscany and Florida, by placing it above a carved gold wood chair, another keepsake.

ABOVE: A favorite hexagonal tray by Hay Copenhagen (known for functional and aesthetic designs) cradles New York MOMA Museum "Glow" tea-light cups atop a garden stool doubling up as a side table.

RIGHT: Though it was encrusted with dirt and treated as a storage area by previous tenants, the screened porch of the formerly run-down cottage turned out to be a surprising find once Kristin and Don began to clean up the derelict space. The hard work revealed a colorful terrazzo floor that would dictate the design of this relaxed bohemian oasis. White furnishings, a high-gloss teal green ceiling, and accents in the same color family reference the proximity of the shimmering waters of the Gulf of Mexico, while verdant areca palms form a natural and lush backdrop. The laid-back, cheerful set-up encourages easy gatherings as chilled as the surroundings. Kristin freely admits to being "somewhat obsessed with one-of-a-kind textiles," as evidenced by the vibrant, color-blocked pillow that was discovered while in Amsterdam at the Lloyd Hotel & Cultural Embassy, a haven for showcasing the work of young artists.

Throughout the home, intriguing and unique finds pepper the rooms with heirloom charm and exoticism. Gifts from the sea, including beachcomber treasures gathered over the years during business trips and personal travels across many continents, speak volumes in this home. Family and friends are intrinsic parts of the décor as well. Photos ranging from simple moments to momentous events and spectacular places highlight shared loves and meaningful occasions.

Kristin finds inspiration from many sources but the one constant is nature. "Blues are the most calming, appealing colors, while green is energizing," she says. Textures also rate highly. "Contrasts create interest. Working high-end design features with lower ones (as illustrated by the union of the custom-made dining table with IKEA chairs) is vitally important to me," she explains. "I like simple with complex. All the senses are textures to be tapped as well. Hearing music or water, experiencing lighting at various levels, moving colors throughout a space—these are all 'texture' devices."

With a lot of elbow grease, a clear understanding of space and function, and a keen eye for beauty and comfort, this cottage has blossomed into a sartorial haven of peace, harmony, and well-being.

The emphasis on simple pleasures must include nature and a sense of light, which is accomplished with a range of coastal whites and watery blues.

OPPOSITE: Situated under the leafy canopy of a shady tree and surrounded by graceful palms, an iconic Lutyens teak bench's masterly proportions and supple curves evoke the very essence of calmness and invite serenity. Indicative of spiritual pursuits, the Buddha head and the stacked stones heighten the secluded spot's meditative aura.

RIGHT: The dreamy setting needs no more than the play of dappled light and the bench, but a soft Tibetan throw (from Arhaus) and a cushy pillow bring maximum comfort when needed. Nature is ultimately the best decorator!

the ARTISTIC BOHEMIAN

Sharlene Kayne is an artist and her family home, nestled in the foothills of the Angeles National Forest in Southern California, is a true reflection of her affinity for art and a representation of her aesthetic. "I don't limit furniture or art to a specific style," she explains. "I like having an eclectic mix because it is personal. I generally collect pieces that I love and meld them together, and it seems to work, and that in turn inspires me."

Sharlene is not formally trained as an artist and, because of that, she says: "there are no rules I have to follow, but it means the learning curve is a lot steeper." However, some of her mother's works played a role in her own creations. "My mother was quite an accomplished painter. She also did some folk art work, and I think the simplicity of that influenced me the most," she notes.

Her own creative endeavors celebrate the handmade and range from soldering to torn-paper collages, newspaper weaving, painting, and jewelry making. That appreciation for all things made by hand combined with numerous trips to foreign lands give her home its unique global flavor.

OPPOSITE: In the dining room, an antique rug found at the Long Beach Flea Market many years ago makes a colorful companion for the kantha throw made from an old sari and repurposed as a tablecloth. Gleaming mercury accents add a seductive shimmer. The pair of vintage wing chairs came with the fun leopard print but Sharlene added the flokati pillows to the smaller chairs, continuing the animal theme. A vintage NYC subway sign adds graphic punch to the room, while the large fiddle-leaf fig tree and other green plants give life and a garden-room feel to the space.

ABOVE LEFT: Sharlene was drawn to the handmade silver Ethiopian crosses for their intricacy and imperfections.

ABOVE CENTER: The elegant, decorative brushes are vintage Japanese calligraphy brushes that Sharlene picked up at an antique store. "I was attracted to the beautiful gem-stone handles," she says.

ABOVE RIGHT: The art above the sideboard—a midcentury-modern piece and a perfect fit for this wall—is the work of Californian artist Agelio Batle, and is made with melted graphite. "I am not sure of the title, but when I saw it I thought of 'See no evil, hear no evil, speak no evil,' although I don't think that was the intention," Sharlene recalls.

PREVIOUS PAGES: In the living room, *The Pearly Queen* by Ann Carrington is given pride of place. The unique piece is made of sewn mother-of-pearl buttons and was a birthday present to Sharlene from her husband Kevin. "I'm attracted to outsider art and art that has an obvious hand touch," she says. "The metal body sculpture was a Rose Bowl Flea Market find, and was $20 as the head was missing," she explains. "I probably wouldn't have bought it if it had the head! But I knew I could rotate different pieces of art above the metal piece, since I have a lot of unusual portrait-style art. The portrait here is a newspaper weaving by Gugger Petter."

ABOVE: True to her love of handmade goods, Sharlene soldered antique crystals to a vintage bottle.

RIGHT: The barrel clay-tile roof, rustic beams, plaster walls, cozy fireplace, and intimate setting come together to create the patio's inherent charm. Sharlene keeps the look simple but comfortable with a black-and-white theme and plenty of plants in burnished copper pots.

OPPOSITE: Sharlene chose to display an old framed silk screen above pillows from diverse sources, including ABC Carpet & Home in NYC, Etsy, and Target. The grouping's warm tones and multi textures set the tone for the room's vibrant and layered look. "I love recycling, and I love upcycling even more," Sharlene says.

ABOVE: When the house was built, this guest bedroom room was originally the master bedroom, hence the fireplace and its border of decorative tiles. "When we moved in, we painted every room with Dunn-Edwards White Heat," says Sharlene, who also made the penny art on the wall next to the fireplace. She creates stunning collages using handmade papers from Japan, India, Nepal, Spain, and Mexico. Fashioned from fabric scraps, the large Moroccan boucherouite rug is another beautiful recycling example.

RIGHT: Set on a wooden tray on the bed's vintage Moroccan kilim, the little beaded horse was made in South Africa by artisans of MonkeyBiz, a company dedicated to reviving the tradition of African beadwork.

"I enjoy frequent traveling, and have been fortunate to visit many countries around the world. A lot of trips were focused on wildlife, including safaris in Kenya, snorkeling in Belize and Tahiti, penguin watching in Australia, and exploring rainforest wildlife in Costa Rica. Trips to other places were more about learning about the great outdoors or cultures, like Iceland, Greece, Turkey, Israel, the Czech Republic, Austria, and Hungary. I spent a fair amount of time touring Europe when my daughter was studying in Paris," she explains.

Sharlene's adventurous and creative spirit is evident throughout her home, and she enjoys moving things around and constantly reinventing her rooms. Currently two of her favorite pieces are given center stage in the main living spaces: a large graphite canvas presides in the dining room and a portrait of Queen Elizabeth, based on a postage stamp—a gift from her husband—oversees the living room.

ABOVE: The master bedroom boasts three walls of windows overlooking numerous trees, a feature Sharlene emphasized by adding plants over the bed using brass plant loops and chains. Kitty Tuco knows a good thing when he sees one, like the lush Moroccan wedding blanket on which he can often be found lounging with the other cats, Phoebe and Eloise. The side tables are vintage brass by Sarreid. Sharlene wanted a pair and was lucky to find one on eBay and a matching one on Etsy. She scored the Peruvian rug at the Melrose Flea Market. A pair of ceramic Brutalist lamps imparts a touch of rusticity to the Zen-like mood of the bedroom. The shades are handmade in the style of classic midcentury fiberglass shades.

An appreciation for all things made by hand, combined with numerous trips to foreign lands, gives her home its unique global flavor.

ABOVE LEFT: Attached to one of the plant hangers is an exquisite Miao Guizhou ceremonial headdress from South China, which Sharlene discovered at the Rose Bowl Flea Market. Within the Miao culture silver adornments are a symbol of wealth, light, and health. It is believed that silver can drive out evil spirits, divert natural disasters, and bring good fortune.

ABOVE RIGHT: Sharlene dressed up the lamps with handmade ceramic bead necklaces she bought in Santorini, Greece. "I don't wear jewelry, but I like my lamps to wear it!" she says.

ABOVE LEFT: Sharlene's daughter Jenna chose Farrow & Ball Cinder Rose paint for the accent wall. "Her favorite color is purple, so the room's many items are variations on the theme," Sharlene explains. The mix of soft and deeper shades, tactile elements, and the unusual chandelier (which required some serious calculations for Jenna and Kevin to hang) conspire to give the space a "midnight at the oasis" kind of vibe.

ABOVE RIGHT: From throws to rugs, pillows to the little furry stool holding the glass cloche cradling a succulent, texture is king in this bedroom. The necklace decoration, handmade from coconut shell from Belize, adds a personal and organic touch.

OPPOSITE: The bed is topped with a vintage kantha quilt layered with a characteristically lustrous, silky, and soft *tulu* rug (a Turkish word meaning "hairy"), which, as the name indicates, is made of the long, curly hair of Angora goats. An abundance of Moroccan pillows are piled high on the bed and on the vintage flokati rug softening the built-in bench below the window. On the walls, both art pieces are more examples of salvaged, repurposed, and framed vintage silk-screen remnants. The floor rug's intricate weave and range of colors echo those of the bedding and pillows and complete the cohesive look.

Sharlene admits that when it comes to decorating, her biggest challenge is that she is attracted to many designs and eras. "I struggle with liking opposites," she explains. "I love color but also neutrals, antiques and modern pieces, curvilinear lines and hard edges, organic and polished. It's finding the balance between all these elements that is the most conflicting."

This multifaceted passion comes to light in every space of her home, but especially in the bedrooms where she indulges her love of fabrics, textures, and colors with abandon. "I love changing the bedding to create mini installations," she says. But overall she is happiest with the master bedroom, due to its warm, rich tones and the view of the treetops. "With three walls of windows it feels like being in a tree house," she says. The guest bedroom and her daughter's room boast an array of brighter colors, tactile elements, and intriguing artisanal pieces brought back from places Sharlene has visited.

Having a love of so many styles could make for a chaotic home, but Sharlene manages to include all in an organized and well-curated look. "Buy and collect things with intention and that really speak to you, and in the end your house will tell the story of you," she concludes.

the **ETHNIC** BOHEMIAN

Kari Payne and her husband John are proof that opposites attract. John is the CEO for a nonprofit organization and Kari is the artistic one. "He's always been analytical," she says. "He's the left-brain type, and I'm definitely more right brain." But when the time came to buy their home in California, they were of the same mind. "We both loved the ranch style, the layout, and the lovely setting," Kari says.

As to her eclectic decorating, Kari is quick to credit her parents. "My family is such a mixture ethnicity-wise, but my parents' all-encompassing styles have had the biggest impact," Kari explains. "My Dad was an interior designer in the 1970s, and my childhood home had old barnwood on the walls and ceilings before reclaimed wood was even a thing. The rooms were filled with Persian rugs, antique cabinets and farm furniture, marble Art Deco tables and mirrors, cow skulls, leaded glass windows, and more. My parents have given me the confidence to mix styles and eras."

It is no wonder that Kari embraces a multitude of genres in her home— from the early simplicity of Native American and the Southwest to the elaborate Spanish and Mediterranean renditions, and more. "I love incorporating things from everywhere, from Morocco to vintage American farmhouse pieces. I think the connecting factor

ABOVE: A modern upholstered bench used as a coffee table brings a sleek, contemporary touch to the living room, yet pairs nicely with the graphic embroidered Otomi pillow from Mexico.

OPPOSITE: Pillows covered in fabrics of varied patterns add texture to the comfy and well-worn leather sofa. Black-and-white photography, a gold-enhanced animal skull, macramé wall hangings, and succulents contribute a subtle, old Southwest feel.

PREVIOUS PAGES: For Kari, the armoire in the living room holds much more than its contents. It was the first piece she and her husband bought together when they married and its value is priceless because it's sentimental, as is the African Bolga basket acquired on a trip to New Orleans for the couple's fifteenth wedding anniversary. The authentic Moroccan floor pillows were a gift from Kari's sister and her husband, who is from Marrakech.

OPPOSITE: Overlaid with an antique handira (a Moroccan wedding blanket), the deep blue wall (painted with Starless Night by Behr) makes a dramatic focal point in the dining room. From the bead chandelier to the table and the bare floor, wood elements keep the room grounded, and the overall look is at once glamorous and earthy. A macramé runner softens the dark wood of the table. The chandelier, a World Market find, was missing some strands of wooden beads, but fortunately Kari had a near exact match from a vintage wood necklace. "I painted the beads to match the existing ones, and it worked perfectly," she explains.

ABOVE LEFT: A wooden cart plays varied roles depending on the occasion—from storing serving pieces to displaying thrifted baskets and plants.

ABOVE RIGHT: The antler, vintage brass tray, candle, vase, and lantern speak of the exotic beauty of a faraway land that complements the mysterious and romantic mood established by the wall-hung Moroccan wedding blanket.

OPPOSITE: In the den, metallic accents from the silver Moroccan leather pouf and the copper side table impart a gentle glow and a lounge vibe. Though disparate in style, the vintage papasan chair, the upholstered pink midcentury chair, and the modern sofa work well together thanks to their hushed colors layered with neutral but textural pillows and throws, like the crochet blanket made by Kari's grandmother. In lieu of art, a Nate Berkus rug takes center stage above the fireplace. The potted cacti themselves are works of art, and black-and-white prints have a strikingly graphic and organic quality. The little bench-turned-coffee table was a gift from a friend. Kari loves pieces with a story because, she says, "It makes your home so much more personal and authentic."

ABOVE LEFT: The large, neutral longhorn skull offers the perfect combination of scale and color to balance the imposing piano. An orphan lamp base found its kin in an ikat shade.

ABOVE RIGHT: The Victorian piano that Kari's mom played in the late 1950s–70s is a stand-alone piece, and one of the family's most treasured possessions. Oversized paper protea flowers—symbol of diversity, courage, and strength—clustered in light and airy macramé by Alicia Siri of Irie Iris Designs, make a soft contrast to the rich wood of the piano. Greenery brings a natural touch without overpowering the peaceful setting.

RIGHT: Kari's friend Jillian, of House of Boys and Beauty, and maker of handmade signs, designed this thoughtful, symbolic sign as a birthday gift for Kari.

"I love incorporating things from everywhere. I think the connecting factor to all these cultures is their rustic, artisanal, and handmade quality."

LEFT: In the entryway, a vintage butcher block on brass casters—a flea-market score—gets dressed up with a macramé runner, driftwood, and potted cacti. True to her favorite art form, Kari keeps her black-and-white prints theme going here. Stacked on a small furry bench, pillows and a blanket herald the home's cozy and welcoming style.

OPPOSITE: "The vignette in my entry was really just a happy accident, but is one of my favorite spots in my home," Kari notes. "I discovered the vintage accordion rack in my grandma's attic and knew it was perfect for my favorite cowboy hat. Then I added the sequined straw bag (which holds dog leashes) and the sun hat, both of which were thrifted. The little handmade macramé piece on driftwood is another favorite, as well as the horseshoe wind chime. When I eventually found the sign, I knew this was the perfect place for it. It reminds me to get out there and live a little!"

LEFT: Kari is quite fond of the "Old West outlaw" vibe and has been collecting faux cow skulls for quite some time. Here one gets embellished with a pompom garland from Mexico.

OPPOSITE: Kari opted to paint the bedroom a warm neutral (Graceful Gray by Behr) because it works well with black and white, "I have always had white bedding because it feels clean and airy and relaxing to me." The addition of black accents happened after she fell in love with a spectacular room featured in an Anthropologie catalog. The striped pillows are a good complement for the black-and-white blanket from her friend and biggest design inspiration, Kate Keesee of Salvage Dior. The bedside lamp, which sits on an antique table, recently received an upgrade with gold spray paint. Over the bed a unique wall hanging features the work of artist Danielle Churchill of RadicalSouls Collective, who makes the tassels by hand and sources the driftwood locally in San Luis Obispo. The simplicity of the piece is the perfect finishing touch for the serene bedroom.

to all these cultures is their rustic, artisanal, and handmade quality," she says. Social media also provides endless inspiration for Kari. "There is such incredible talent online," she recognizes. The most notable impact came from the relationship she and her friend Kate Keesee (of Salvage Dior) formed via Instagram. "Kate's instinct for creating beautiful spaces using only reclaimed items and pieces from thrift shops is pure magic."

Travels also influence her approach to décor. "We recently visited Mexico and New Orleans, and were captivated by the architecture and sense of history in both places." Kari says. "I love warm, cozy interiors with a mixture of rustic and modern, and a collected, eclectic vibe. To me it's relaxing and inspiring all at once."

Kari's home is always evolving, though she has some items she says are here to stay. "My antique wood furniture pieces are my favorite because they stand the test of time and work with so many different styles, regardless of the current trends."

It is clear that Kari favors items with interesting stories and various pedigrees. "Take your time and combine what you love," she advises. "Design your home to be unique and personal to you, and a reflection of your life. That is what really makes a house a home."

the *the* **TROPICAL** SPIRIT

Set like a jewel in the Gulf of Mexico, Florida's Anna Maria Island is a short drive from Tampa or Orlando, via a bridge which links it to the mainland. Arriving on this tropical 7-mile strip of land feels like you've landed in paradise, according to those who know about this well-kept secret.

Kandice Ridley spent a good part of her childhood living an hour from the island, enjoying weekends and vacations there with her family. Although she married a Texan and moved to Dallas, she and her husband David continued to visit the island frequently. In 2007, the couple bought a small bungalow on Anna Maria Island, for the family to use as a vacation home. It was formerly the guesthouse for an adjacent waterfront beach house. "The tiny home hadn't been updated since being built in the 1940s. Staying there was like stepping back in time," says Kandice, who got to work transforming the forlorn house into the boho gem she had in mind: a mix of elements from Hawaii, the California coast, and classic Florida beach houses.

To expand the original square footage and accommodate an additional bedroom and bathroom, Kandice and David added the upper level. The gable was ornamented with a gingerbread border and a wave-like trim under the roofline. The ground-level

ABOVE: A vintage tablecloth gets a new life as a pillow cover that pays tribute to the sunshine state and the cottage's roots.

OPPOSITE: Kandice found the weathered shutters in a salvage yard and had them added to the living-room wall along with the shingles, to give the room the appearance that it was once an outside wall. The lamp was a secondhand find to which she added the Hawaiian hula-style raffia shade. The original floor was stained to complement the newly repainted room.

PREVIOUS PAGES: Vibrant colors, quirky mismatched furnishings, kitschy accessories, and a variety of patterns —from striped pillows to chairs upholstered in tribal motifs, and an armchair and couch revamped with custom fabrics—give the living room its tropical punch.

LEFT: Though disparate in styles and eras, the aqua Formica countertop, the painted and distressed cabinets and the open-fronted sink with its pink trim seem to be made for each other. The look is positively joyful!

OPPOSITE: If proof of Kandice's love affair with seaside colors and fun objects was needed, the kitchen would put any doubt to rest. The room is awash in blue, aqua, and teal and almost every surface holds a playful piece, may it be a graphic old storage tin, a tree made from pieces of driftwood, a painted sign, or a shell-embellished bottle. The shelves and trim were made by local woodworkers to reflect the gulf waves. "The table and chairs were my grandmother's," Kandice recalls. "I grew up eating at that table and it brings back many great memories. I wanted the kitchen to be reminiscent of the 1950s with a fun, eclectic twist, hence the fridge and stove, both reproductions."

porch was given railings and architectural brackets to blend in with the new addition. Kandice played with several colors until she zeroed in on exactly what she had in mind and then dry-brushed the paint with a very light blue tint to create an aged look and add character.

"For both the exterior and interior, my true inspiration was nature," she says. "All the colors are drawn from ocean sea glass, the skies at different times of day, rainbows, foliage, and the amazing plumage of island birds. I ended up using 38 different colors!" Spirited fabrics, fanciful accessories, exotic furnishings, and nature-inspired colors influenced by the tropical seaside location set the tone for carefree family times in the beach retreat. "Creating a cozy feel was my number-one goal," Kandice explains. "For an informal room that looks well planned out, mixing a variety of colors, fabrics, and textures does the trick as long as you always include the same shades of one color to pull it all together."

Today, three generations of the family share the well-kept secret that is Anna Maria Island. It's their own little piece of paradise. "I spent months searching for architectural salvage, art that spoke to me, and unique fabrics. But, what makes a house truly your own is filling it with family memories."

ABOVE: For true wow factor, you could not beat a statement piece like this bed, inspired by gifts from the deep and dressed in a spectrum of watery shades. For such a dazzling headboard, nothing less than the equally exuberant bedspread and intensely colorful pillows would do. Kandice found the bed in a local junk store and proceeded to transform it with aquatic treasures into a one-of-a-kind piece worthy of even the pickiest of mermaids, one of which graces the pillow atop a quartet of others in jewel colors. The sign over the bed sums up Kandice's affection for the cottage. The vibrant seaweed-color papier-mâché fish and the fun lampshade leave no doubt as to the coastal location.

LEFT: The headboard's original wicker panels are layered with numerous shells of different varieties and sizes, including starfish, beaded periwinkle, Florida cone, whelks, conch, urchins, and sand dollars, as well as sea glass. In lieu of pearls, the garland of clam shells holds gem-like sea glass in frosted colors.

"All the colors are drawn from the ocean sea glass, the skies at different times of the day, rainbows, foliage, and the amazing plumage of island birds."

ABOVE LEFT: The upstairs bedroom opens up to a balcony overlooking the beach and the turquoise and azure waters of the Gulf of Mexico. Below the balcony, where grass meets sand, a trio of bright pink chairs provides the perfect spot to meditate in the first morning light or take in the magnificent sunsets at day's end.

ABOVE RIGHT: Kandice has collected mermaids from souvenir stores and flea markets for years. "They are a link to our home away from home and to four generations of a beach-loving family," she says.

RIGHT: The whitewashed floor of the new bedroom mimics the sandy beach, while the pale yellow walls and ceiling recall the soft sunlight that bathes the room in the early morning. A duvet cover with a hummingbird and floral pattern and a beaded trim brings comfort and charm to the bleached-wood bed. Kandice relies on local stores for decorative items like the painting over the bed, the collection of mermaids found throughout the cottage, and accessories, including the urn lamp and the fish vase on the desk, painted by one of the island's artists.

LEFT: Intricately carved brackets and doors from India give a mysterious, temple-like look to the entrance to the bathroom. Vintage and modern come together in the dresser-turned-vanity, fitted with a contemporary sink. The tiny chandelier strung with amber crystals adds a chic boho touch.

ABOVE: Shells and sea glass collected on the island are a recurring decorating staple and theme in one form or another throughout this seaside home.

OPPOSITE: True to her love of nature, for the exterior of the family's storybook cottage Kandice chose shades of aqua and blue to reflect the nearby Gulf of Mexico. Fretwork painted green recalls the surrounding verdant foliage and gentle waves, while hot pink Adirondack chairs add brilliant contrast to the deep turquoise of the table.

the WANDERER

When Sarah Caliguri and her husband Matt were looking for a place to set down roots, Carlsbad, California was the answer to their quest. "Not only is it one of the nicest beach towns in this area, but the community and village are so quaint and unique," Sarah explains. "It has the ultimate artsy-surf-beachy vibe." These were deciding factors, as she is a nature lover and Matt a surfer. They settled on a particular apartment because, as Sarah says, "Even though it's not large, it feels spacious, and I love that it is on the top floor and that the balcony faces west so we can sit outside and watch the sunsets, and we love being only two miles from the sea."

Upon entering the couple's home it is evident that Sarah is neither a minimalist nor timid when it comes to style and color. "I love global goods and vivid hues," she admits. "Nature, places I have visited, and cultures are a constant source of inspiration." One of these trips was for their honeymoon. "We went to Costa Rica and stayed at a retreat on the beach in Santa Teresa, which is on the Nicoya Peninsula and is known for its amazing surf and yoga classes," Sarah recalls. "It definitely inspired my boho surf-shack style: lots of good vibes, natural wood, tropical plants, fun art, seashells, and bright colors."

ABOVE: Made by skilled craftsmen in India, the mango-wood table with a burned wax finish holds clay coasters that have been glazed to a glassy sheen. A tropical bromeliad nestles in a basket woven from palms and banana leaves.

OPPOSITE: In the living room, the array of pillows is always in a state of flux. "I'm constantly changing them and the light gray sofa provides the perfect neutral base," Sarah explains. "I can add faux fur, tassels, fringe, or African mudcloth in with solid colors or other patterns. I like to have the bigger pillows in the corners and then smaller ones in the center. The main colors throughout our home are pinks, greens, teal, and blues."

ABOVE: To give the living room its beachy, tropical, earthy ambiance, Sarah selected an intoxicating range of hues, patterns, embellishments, and eclectic furnishings and accessories. The room is on the small size, but that didn't deter Sarah from creating a cohesive, and comfortable space to accommodate family and friends without feeling crowded. "Having room for dance parties with my girlfriends was also a must!" she insists. "I wanted to achieve a laid-back, layered bungalow-meets-lounge feel." The ample sofa piled with a fusion of ethnic and folksy pillows, the elegant tufted chair, and the carved wood coffee table set atop layered rugs accomplish her goal. Sarah added the brass skull and sprigs of faux flowers to impart more layers and an organic quality is provided by a natural fiber woven jute rug used as a wall hanging. The gold lantern and cactus on the shelf tie in with the skull.

OPPOSITE LEFT: Sarah's trek to Bali inspired the colors and items she displays in the hallway niche. "The unforgettable experience compelled me to have one colorful wall in my home and this small recess was the perfect spot. It reminds me of being surrounded by the lush foliage from the jungles. This paint color is Green Suede by Valspar."

OPPOSITE RIGHT: The blue hutch was found as is. "I love the color because it ties in nicely with my beachy décor," says Sarah, who grew up on the coast and spends her free time relaxing and meditating on the beach. The vintage sign appealed to her for what she calls "its surf-shack character."

Plants are a major component of bohemian décor and Sarah includes many and varied ones, whether hanging or in pots, to keep the iconic look flowing from room to room.

Another faraway destination, a trip to Bali, made a particularly lasting impression on Sarah "I was completely charmed by the kaleidoscope of colors, mischievous monkeys, fresh fruit, vendors offerings exotic goods along the paths, the smell of incense burning, chanting from the nearby temples, and the surrounding lush jungle. It was a spiritual experience that truly captivated me."

Looking back, Sarah says her style has always been bohemian. "I have always liked gleaning things from various sources, from small shops to large ones—especially from my favorites: Anthropologie, World Market, and Home Goods—specialty boutiques, thrift stores, and flea markets. I love shopping and global décor has become so available and affordable, which is fabulous when you can't travel as much as you would like. I also have a lot of things passed on from my family. It is more of a lifestyle," she explains "My husband and I are unconventional and like doing things our own way, not following what others do or what is expected. To me, a bohemian home is free-spirited, incorporates travel and family, mixed in with soulful gypsy vibes; I love that it doesn't follow the norms and stands out from traditional or trendy looks."

OPPOSITE: A Balinese-style sideboard, a gift from a friend, sports an intricate macramé runner similar in texture to the small wall hanging Sarah brought back from Bali. The cactus cookie jar and matching salt-and-pepper set are especially dear to her because they belonged to her grandmother. "She got them from a local shop on one her desert vacations in Arizona." Baskets of all shapes, sizes, and colors can be found throughout the house. "I love how each one shows a pretty design and can be used as a display on the wall or for planters or bowls in the kitchen or on tables. They are not only attractive and versatile but also very practical!" she says. The clay skull came home with Sarah from a birthday trip to Sedona, Arizona. Always the nature lover, she adorned it with a flower crown.

ABOVE: A crackled ceramic pot and a glass jar filled with colorful sand form an oasis for the little llama, one of several endearing residents of the hutch.

RIGHT: A green rattan wicker hutch from a local thrift store provides plenty of display space for colorful bowls and whimsical creatures. "I love to include camels, giraffes, elephants, and llamas in my space. They make you feel like you are in a faraway place, like Morocco or India," Sarah says. Above the hutch, a green-and-gold candle lantern projects a pretty mandala pattern on the ceiling when lit.

"I love global goods and vivid hues. Nature, places I have visited, and cultures are a constant source of inspiration."

LEFT: With budget restrictions in mind, the ever-resourceful Sarah applied a look-alike subway tile contact paper to conceal the sides of an unsightly island and brighten up the tiny kitchen that has no window or natural light. To add yet more charm and interest, she removed some of the cabinet doors, allowing her unique plates, bowls, and glassware to become part of the personal décor. "They are also so much fun to rearrange," she says.

OPPOSITE: With perky colors, mixed textures, and eye-catching details, Sarah managed to transform a run-of-the-mill eating area into a seductive dining alcove. A handmade runner from Mexico proved irresistible "The colors of the embroidered flowers are magical," she muses. Artwork collected from worldwide artists is enhanced with tassels and pompom garlands, including a custom piece made by Sarah's friend, fiber artist Jody@six1one. The right lighting makes all the difference to a room, and here the brass pendant and string lights make the space come alive with a mystical glow.

OPPOSITE: Mismatched furnishings, like this wood chest of drawers and wicker shelves, exemplify the unscripted nature of bohemian style, but objects of similar nature and significance—like baskets, plants, and animal and spiritual sculptures—connect the two pieces.

ABOVE LEFT: Australian textile designer Cassie Byrnes conceptualized the bedspread of colorful flower silhouettes. "I love the cheerful jungalow mood it brings to our bedroom," Sarah says. The pink Berber wool rug echoes the many sunset hues of the pillows, and Sarah's innate sense of color and style combinations shines in this pillow grouping. "I mix and match patterns that typically might not go together for an eclectic, bohemian style. I like to be bold and have fun with doing the unexpected for a unique and one-of-a-kind look." Instead of a headboard, Sarah chose a room divider constructed with hand-woven macramé panels framed in mango wood. "I love its warm bohemian chic," she explains. "I like using pieces for purposes other than their intended function. As a headboard, it adds depth and texture against the blank wall, and I layered on a colorful tassel garland." Also on display is another piece by Sarah's friend Jody, a hand-woven wall hanging. "I love her use of colors," says Sarah.

ABOVE CENTER: Buddha plays an important role for Sarah. "I have many around our home. They are reminders of his spiritual practices of compassion and the power of now. Meditation and yoga are a huge part of my life and I enjoy creating sacred altars for daily rituals," she explains. The rose quartz "love-romance stone" is placed in front of Buddha to create the ultimate feng shui. This crystal vibrates energy of unconditional love, joy, and healing. It is known to open the heart chakra to all forms of love and is believed to raise self-esteem and balance emotions. To maximize the good energy it emits, the bedroom is the favorite location.

ABOVE RIGHT: Storage is in short supply in the apartment. Sarah could have easily enclosed the bedroom's existing open shelving area or replaced the lower shelves with a dresser, but instead she chose to make it part of the bedroom décor and turn it into an attractive and organized stage for baskets filled with small items like belts, scarves, and socks.

OVERLEAF: Sarah's vagabond spirit rules the guest bedroom. Packed with color, textiles, and ephemera, it resembles the choreographed chaos and delightful mix of India's bazaars or Morocco's souks. From the rattan headboard to the multihued pillows and the African mudcloth throw, the space boasts an exotic and free-spirited atmosphere. Sarah made the wall hanging from yarn, driftwood, and feathers, and embellished a stick she found on a walk. "I like to bring in natural elements for their earthy quality, using them as accents or to hang plants or strings of lights." Though a long way from home, the elephant bench from India is perfectly suited for the room. A bejeweled elephant and the glow of a silver pot and gold candle impart a hint of intrigue and a touch of luster.

Her decor embraces that philosophy with a mix of beach-house and tropical-island styles, with Indian, Moroccan, and Turkish influences thrown in, and plenty of energizing, yet relaxing and refreshing, pinks, greens, and blues. "When I walk into our home, I want to feel I am entering a cozy sanctuary. Incense is always burning, music playing, little lights twinkling, essential oils wafting, and wine ready to be served. After a long shift, I enjoy coming home to my refuge," she says.

Her spiritual side also comes into focus, which for Sarah, a psychiatric nurse working with older patients, provides relief from her demanding job. She creates little altars where Buddha is placed in the center along with sage, crystals, incense, candles, and Palo Santo sticks. "It brings me instant peace and gratitude. Life is all about moderation and balance," she explains. "It's about embracing love, laughter, comfort, and adventures." And Sarah and Matt's home exemplifies that positive and balanced lifestyle.

ABOVE: Little lounging and reading spots are set up within the guest bedroom to provide a variety of areas to relax. An ottoman overlaid with a tropical leaf motif and topped with comfy pillows sits under a trio of hanging plants, creating a garden-room mood. The ladder was a project Sarah and her mom made together to store and display blankets. "The plaster zodiac sign was my grandma's," Sarah says. "She painted it a copper color and I lightened it up a little with some gold shimmer paint. I love astrology, so this piece is very sentimental to me."

OPPOSITE: The rattan peacock chair is a favorite find, which Sarah calls "a beautiful goddess statement piece." Including artwork from various artists with whom she connected on Instagram is very meaningful to Sarah. "I love art from women of different ethnic backgrounds, to show unity and oneness."

OPPOSITE: A faux-fur rug adds softness and comfort to the wire chair. The small open-shelved unit was once part of an old desk and is now a favorite spot for Sarah to create ever-changing vignettes. Presently it is home to colorful baskets, prints, plants, and some of Sarah's books on physical and emotional well-being.

ABOVE: Day or night, the balcony always glows thanks to a radiant disco ball sparkling in the sunlight and the flickering of candle-lit lanterns at night.

RIGHT: Even the smallest spots don't escape Sarah's original and personal touches. She transformed a narrow balcony off the living room into her private little jungle. "The bench and tropical plants remind me of our trips to Costa Rica and Bali," she recalls. She treated the space as one would an indoor room by adding art in the form of a wall hanging, a shutter mimicking a window, a rug for added warmth and texture, and bamboo fencing for privacy and style.

the SCANDI BOHEMIAN

"My mother always told me to stick to 'jewel tones' and she was correct! Imagine that!" laughs Erin Barrett, the maven designer behind Sunwoven, the handmade textile company she founded in Charleston, South Carolina.

In 2015, Erin and her husband Creighton, the drummer for the indie-rock group Band of Horses, were in search of a large home that could accommodate both his and hers studios and their growing family. Luckily, a spacious 3,600-square foot ranch-style house came on the market and they jumped at the chance to grab the circa 1970s house. "Just like my work, I knew how I wanted our home to feel more than how I wanted it to look," Erin recalls. "There were a lot of things that we loved about this house, but the layout, the light, and the sunken living room were the biggest reasons we chose it."

Erin and Creighton are both fans of the clean lines of Scandinavian designs and of the California-coast surf style, and are very inspired by color and natural light. They entertain a lot and, as Erin says, "The large open spaces and high ceilings make for a perfect place to host a dinner party or small get-together. We see this house as not only our

ABOVE LEFT: Whether taking in the view of the garden or enjoying listening to Creighton at the piano, the California-cool hanging woven rattan chair in the living room is the place to be. Surrounding greenery and textural accents add comfort and exotic touches.

ABOVE RIGHT: Located in a den, just a few steps from the dining room, a cozy spot is outfitted with a midcentury-modern chair and lamp. The pillow is one of many from Sunwoven, Erin's textile company.

OPPOSITE: Erin and Creighton wanted to maximize the natural light pouring into the living room and give it a fresh, modern vibe typical of Scandinavian style. "A lot of what we did was cosmetic," Erin says. "We painted the pecky cypress walls white and replaced the dark flooring with a natural birch engineered hardwood. It makes everything in the room pop." The chandelier was only supposed to be a temporary fixture until Erin could find one that she really liked, but it became a keeper. "I have grown to like this affordable version!" she notes. Creighton had always wanted a space to display his surfboards. "They are not technically art pieces, but they are art to us," Erin says. "I love what they bring to the space and how they tell a story. Creighton uses them every week."

ABOVE: Shaped like a ship's hull, the table hints at Creighton's affection for water and his love of surfing. Who says art has to be limited to what's hanging on your walls? Erin spruces up the sofa with gallery-worthy pillows showcasing stripes, geometric patterns, and fringe trims in neutral hues.

RIGHT: "I had always wanted a dining room set that would seat everyone, including children, when we had guests over for meals," explains Erin. "This extending oak table and the beech wood chairs allow for twelve people comfortably, which is perfect as we love to entertain." Erin chose the fireplace screen for its design. "It's more unique than others I had seen and it is interesting to the eye," she notes. At the side of the sofa, the colorful basket, found in a local plant shop, not only complements the warm color scheme but also provides useful storage. Set against the far wall, the piano was a gift to Creighton from his best friend for his fortieth birthday. "We had always wanted one, so this was really a gift for the whole family," Erin says. Above the piano, the couple gave famed musician David Bowie a place of honor, not only because of his body of work but as Erin says, "We have always loved this photo of David Bowie. In fact, he is our son's namesake; also, I love the yellow suit!"

"My style has always been boho, but lately it's evolved to include Scandinavian influences and more modern lines."

LEFT: A cozy throw and cushy pillows top one of two midcentury-modern sofas (from Gus Modern). A versatile rattan pouf serves as an extra seat or a coffee table. An abundance of healthy plants connect the room to nature and the gardens beyond. Erin waited until she could find the perfect piece of art to hang over the fireplace. "I knew it was the right one when I came across it," she says. "It's unlike anything I have seen before, and the gold foil adds a fun element to the room and ties in with the side table from Target." The shaggy tribal rug from Home Goods brings a graphic touch and anchors the room. A framed typographic print on the hearth spells out Erin's motto.

OPPOSITE: When remodeling the kitchen, shiplap was added to the side of the bar facing the family room. "It needed texture and also to tie in with the paneling in the living room. We decided to make a bold move and paint it charcoal (Ebony Field by Valspar)," Erin recalls. "It immediately transformed the space and connected it with the rest of the house." The bar stools' low profile allows an uninterrupted view of the dining room and living room, which Erin truly enjoys. "We can be in the kitchen without feeling isolated or unable to see the action happening in the rest of the house!"

ABOVE: In the master bedroom, the charcoal wall allows the large wood headboard, made by Creighton, to become the focal point, together with a pillow and throw from Erin's Sunwoven company. Though kept to a minimum, decorative accents in brass and copper contribute a rich, warm glow. The light green hues of the drapes and sheers establish a connection with the plants and the garden. Erin is known for her handwoven wall hangings and textiles, and the ones displayed here are from the collection she created for Anthropologie. "The inspiration for the textiles came from 'organic' style weaving, our most popular style and a signature look for Sunwoven," she explains. "Color was important and we spent a lot of time putting together color combinations, which of course included gold metallic ribbon. Once the colorways were decided, I made a few different wall hangings that worked as prototypes and inspiration for what the product has now become."

OPPOSITE LEFT: One of Erin's wall hangings and a tasseled chandelier (by Justina Blakeney for Anthropologie) endow the bedroom's reading spot with definite boho attitude.

OPPOSITE RIGHT: The master bathroom received a modern makeover complete with white subway-tiled walls, a graphite-hued ceramic floor, and copper fixtures that lifted it from boring to soothing, with the Zen vibe that spas are known for. The deep tub with its wooden caddy, candle, and plant is the perfect spot to indulge in a relaxing soak, while the shower is the place to go to feel invigorated.

home, but also the place where we both work and draw inspiration from." She adds, "My style has always been boho, but lately it's evolved to include Scandinavian influences and more modern lines." She skillfully blends the various aesthetics by uniting sleek midcentury pieces with streamlined Scandinavian accents, and introducing cool boho accessories in a way that embraces each style and makes the home look pulled together and welcoming.

"We became more and more interested in interior design with our previous house, but really made an effort and poured our hearts into our current home to create a space that was a true reflection of ourselves and our family," Erin explains, "I love that our rooms aren't overly busy or cluttered, but still have heart and meaning."

When it came to establishing a color palette, Erin felt a little conflicted. "I get torn because I'm drawn to clean white minimalism, but both Creighton and I also love color," she says. "As you can clearly see, I did heed my mother's words: yellow is one of my biggest color inspirations. Not only is it cheerful but it's also calming, and really catches the eye and brings joy." True to their affection for the bright hue, pops of the happy color—from furnishings to accessories and art— enliven the living room with their sunny disposition.

There's no doubt Erin and Creighton have found their happy place. "I like a space that's bright and fresh, open and airy, and clean and modern." Erin explains. "Maintaining a comfortable, family-friendly home while keeping true to our design aesthetic is something that we are always striving to achieve." The results speak for themselves.

the ROMANTIC BOHEMIAN

You could say I am a gypsy at heart, yet at the same time I am a true homebody.

I have a wonderful job. I travel a lot with hundreds of trips from coast to coast and every state in between, get to meet lovely people, and style interiors for photo shoots. That alone is an endless source of inspiration, but when you add in visits to several continents, it's easy to see how all this globetrotting has fueled my own wanderlust! I always return to my home in Florida with fresh ideas and plenty of sweet souvenirs, and that is why the look of my home is ever-changing.

As we know too well, it's hard to limit yourself to just one style when so many beguiling options are available, and so easily attainable. That flexibility and affordability are what make bohemian décor so appealing to me. My home has become a lab for experimenting with colors, furniture placement, and displays of found and favorite objects. I like rooms to tell a story, but also feel playful yet restful. When creating a space, I think about the places I have visited and the memories they hold, such as evocative colors and fragrances, then I try to adapt those to my own lifestyle.

While I love vivid and cheerful hues in other people's home, I prefer a softer palette for my own. I find that after being on the road, I need a soothing and peaceful environment where I can reflect on everything I have seen, and also regroup. In addition, a soft palette makes a beautiful backdrop to layer with personal items. I have

ABOVE: I have boxes of props left over from photo shoots, including quite a collection of napkin rings as varied in styles as they are in colors and materials. This pink sequined one glistens like jewelry and is the perfect accessory for a festive occasion.

OPPOSITE: I don't have a proper dining room so the kitchen is where I host small dinner parties. Here I kept to my favorite blue and pink palette, choosing deeper tones for a livelier mood. I looked high and low for a fabric lantern to hang over the table but with no success, so I made my own with a remnant of pink lace and added a flirty fringe, pompoms, and a sparkly trim. The tablecloth is actually a light cotton throw. I have a thing for metallics, such as the brass bar cart. Used sparingly, shiny objects add life to a room. Mixing glassware of different sizes and colors is so very boho!

PREVIOUS PAGES: In my living room I wanted to create an uncomplicated and dreamy mood, and beautiful blues always have that effect on me. Adding a few discreet pops of pinks helps unite the alcove and the main living room area. The wood-bead chandelier was originally teal in color, but I painted it white to fit in with the subdued palette. Light cotton curtains are trimmed with pompoms, a hallmark of boho décor. Details are the icing on the decorating cake. Gold touches—from the table base to the glass candleholder, the rim of the vase, and the elephant—impart a touch of luxury without overpowering the tranquil setting. Since I don't have a room I can dedicate to meditation, to the left of the sofa I set up a small corner with candles grouped on a Lucite table under a mirror that reflects the natural light during the day and enhances the candles' glow at night. Though simple, it is arranged altar-style to promote mindfulness rituals.

RIGHT: To me, fondant shades of pale pinks and soft blues are simply delicious. Subtle colors are soothing and create a cohesive look, so I painted the floor a light gray and finished with a whitewash to complement rather than compete with the pink accent wall. The circular pink stool brings a softness that a square or rectangular table wouldn't. Rugs and pillows with similar patterns and in the same color family add luscious layers to the room's informality. I fell in love with a linen remnant's graceful design and had it made into a slipcover for the wing chair. There isn't much need for a fireplace in Florida, but I wanted one as it heightens the coziness quotient of any room. The silver-leaf candleholders on the mantelpiece are French and the large straw tassel on the hearth is from Africa. The painted walking stick doesn't hail from so far away, being made by Florida artist Laura Dellaporta. In a small home mirrors and other reflective surfaces play a big role in adding dimension and sparkle, hence the collection of mirrors. I don't have a lot of wall space, but I like to feature artwork wherever possible, especially portraits because they make a room come alive.

ABOVE: When storage space is at a premium, one has to get creative and, as the saying goes, "necessity is the mother of invention!" I always loved this slender console for its shape and versatility, having used it as a desk, a room divider, and now to display favorite objects. It had been painted over many times, until I discovered Ralph Lauren's line of metallic paints several years ago and was instantly seduced by this rosy hue called Fairy Circle. It has remained that pearly pale pink color ever since. When I reconfigured the living room, I ended up not having a spot for the ottoman that was used as a coffee table in its former life. Tucking it under the console was the solution to make use of the empty space beneath and supply much-needed room for some of the many books I often refer to for ideas and inspiration.

OPPOSITE LEFT: Objects and accessories can be used to highlight a style or enhance a mood, but for me the ones that matter are those with personal significance and emotional value. Hearts are my favorite and can be seen in every room. My very first one was a gift from my mother, when I was in my teens, and since then I have collected them from all over the world. They are such a lovely symbol and pairing them with a Buddha, who embodies peace and gratitude, is a match made in heaven, or in this case, Nirvana. A curated collection of storied hearts holds memories of the places I have visited and the people who gave them to me. Some are more valuable than others, but all are priceless. The embellished horseshoe was a thoughtful good luck gift, and placing it among the hearts was an obvious choice.

OPPOSITE RIGHT: Grouped on top of the console, the lantern's lace-like filigree pattern, the pink frosted vase, the iridescent shells, and the small fuchsia votive infuse the space with romance and warmth.

been described as a romantic and fought that label for a long time until I took a good look around my home and came to the conclusion that it does, in fact, show my true spirit.

Yes, there is no point denying it: the overall feel is gentle and, well, romantic. I admit that hearts are my greatest weakness! I love elements that have a human connection to them. They bring a unique dimension and an artful addition to any space. And look at that sofa! I had wanted a "glamorous" one for such a long time but every one I saw was incredibly expensive, until the day I walked into Home Goods and there it was: a plush, silvery-blue, cushy, curvy chesterfield just waiting for me, and for a song! And just to add a further layer of romance to my living room, I installed a fireplace strictly for its seductive appeal, proving the point that at heart I am a romantic.

Whatever your boho dream décor, reinventing or simply rethinking your rooms is easily accomplished with a few changes, may it be through color, furnishings, or accessories, and the best part is that it need not cost a fortune or require you to travel the world over either. Stores like Home Goods, Anthropologie, World Market, and Target offer worldly, exotic goods for a fraction of the cost of a trip to Bali or Morocco. Flea markets and garage sales are also good bets: you can find some spectacular items at a price that's hard to beat. Indulging your decorating passions, your lust for adventure, and your inner gypsy makes for an exciting interior.

My home is a work in progress because there will always be new pieces to fall in love with, though sentimental ones, like paintings by friends and gifts received while on shoots, will always remain key elements of my personal style. Everything in my home is meant to be touched—and meant to touch you. Each piece has its own meaningful story. And every time I come back from a trip, I fall in love with my little house all over again. My home is my cocoon and it makes my heart sing!

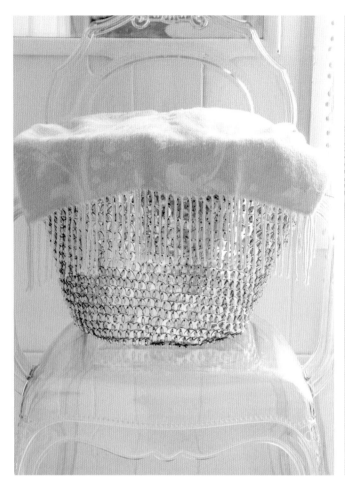

ABOVE LEFT: In a corner of the bedroom, a see-through acrylic chair prevents the small space from feeling crowded and allows a handmade Moroccan silver basket to star, while providing neat storage for a collection of belts.

ABOVE RIGHT: An antique French mirror hangs above a zinc garden table. Grouped together, a "love totem" by artist Sandra Evertson, a curvy frosted bottle wearing a shell garland and a bead necklace with a clay heart, and a Moroccan glass whisper gently of the sea, love, and exotic places, rather than shout.

OPPOSITE: I love living on the coast. The seaside engages all the senses and allows the mind to float free. So it comes as no surprise that turning the bedroom into a soothing sanctuary was a must. Indigo skies, azure waters, and white wispy clouds inspire the hues and finishes for a look that is easy on the eye and gentle on the psyche. White is known to establish a calm environment but too much of it can easily become cold and soulless, so the light shibori throw keeps the white comforter from overpowering the bed. The many shades of blues cohabit happily with each other and provide the common thread for varied textures and patterns. The lighter blues of the fluffy Mongolian fur and the natural shibori hemp pillows balance the deeper hues of the glossy Indian silk on either side. In typical bohemian fashion, no two pieces are identical. A tall sideboard on one side of the bed and a zinc table on the other take the place of traditional nightstands. Mirrors also have their own identity. Though disparate in size and finishes, a pair of brass hearts, found in different parts of the country, makes a united and romantic statement above the bed. Next to the window, a dreamy portrait by artist Cindy Redman is all about softness and femininity, while voile curtains diffuse the light, giving the room an ethereal glow. The statement rug kicks up the visual contrast a notch.

ABOVE: Bracelets, necklaces, and rings—some vintage, some new, and collected from many countries—drip from a sculptural hand. Once used by glovemakers, this hand is a work of art in its own right and deserves to be shown, not hidden.

RIGHT: The old dresser has served several functions and seen many colors over the years but, like a chameleon, it is highly adaptable to its surrounding. In its current incarnation it doubles as a vanity. The golden mirror above it communicates the brilliance of the Florida sun. Candles are scattered throughout and lit regularly, making fragrance an indispensable element of the décor. When I couldn't find the kind of unique artwork I wanted for my bedroom wall, I decided to make one myself and created a collage by selecting favorite images from photo shoots I have been on. If you look closely, you will see it also includes lots of hearts, words, and even some pieces of broken jewelry to make it more three dimensional. The process of creating this was akin to a spiritual pilgrimage.

The concept for this little garden retreat was to create an outdoor room sheltered from both the hot Florida sun and summer downpours, as well has being an eclectic and beguiling little haven. It is situated only steps from my house, so it needed to fit in with the existing architecture yet have its own identity.

Establishing the sense of comfortable enclosure was key to achieving the look successfully and, to that effect, making use of the existing high fence, a tin roof set on posts was added to a corner of the patio. A scalloped ledge, found on the side of the road, accentuates and dresses up the front.

The little sanctuary delivers a multisensory experience through the visually calming décor, the aural presence of gently pealing wind chimes, the comforting feel of fabrics, the taste of refreshing sweet tea, and the heady perfume of roses mingling with the lemony fragrance of moonflowers. Bohemians often find inspiration in nature and, true to the style, it is one of the key decorating aesthetics for this outdoor oasis. Adding to the narrative, potted plants, exuberant bougainvillea, and climbing vines are a lovely stylistic expression defining the entrance naturally and effortlessly.

Old and new furnishings are kept within a range of white hues to complement the peaceful setting and celestial blues heighten its restorative essence. Though a mini version of a Zen retreat, this tiny oasis is big on encouraging meditation and mindfulness.

PREVIOUS PAGES: My garden retreat was designed to allow me to spend time outside on the patio, sheltered from the sun and the summer downpours. The space is furnished with an eclectic mix of secondhand furniture, united by a fresh coat of white paint to create a serene and calm mood. Accessories are connected to each other by various shade of blue. Colored-glass lanterns from discount stores and hanging crystal votives that have been upcycled from broken light fixtures give the space a bit of glitz and glamour. Wispy sheers and climbing vines frame the setting and contribute to the sense of privacy. A little altar has been created on the circular table, with a few palm fronds, sprigs from a flowering vine, and a profusion of votives offering a peaceful spot for a serene Buddha and a moment of introspection. A capiz wind chime provides a gentle musical background.

OPPOSITE LEFT: A former pot rack finds a new purpose as the keeper of personal and meaningful objects.

OPPOSITE RIGHT: Nature is a key element of the bohemian aesthetic and is often featured in unique and personal ways, from colorful pots to animal-inspired containers. A heart and antlers enliven the table with the warmth of burnished gold.

RIGHT: A narrow bench, plump floor cushions, and a little stool offer seating options without taking up a lot of space. The mirror acts as a "window," amplifying the natural light and adding depth and dimension. The old farm table was cut down to a coffee-table height to fit the laid-back style of this nook. A hemp pillow brings comfort to a wooden bench and a pair of shibori curtains creates a wall-like separation between the outdoor room and the steps to the entrance of the house. An old repainted column turned out to be the perfect fit for a tight corner, providing a plinth for a Moroccan lantern.

the **BEACH** BOHEMIAN

Some things in life are simply meant to be. Lisa and Mario De Pinto weren't looking for a beach cottage. They were quite content (or so they thought) living on one of Florida's more touristy islands when destiny sent Lisa on an errand, directing her over the historic one-lane swing bridge to Casey Key, a barrier island on the Gulf of Mexico.

"I literally took a sigh of relief," she recalls. "I found myself on this quiet, meandering road in a place with no high-rise condos or even one traffic light." After countless trips to experience the tranquil beauty of the key first hand and to drive by a home that the couple named Pink Shell Cottage—"because the color reminded us of the inside of a conch shell," Lisa says—they bought the house and moved to Casey Key. "I had the overwhelming feeling that I was home."

The property came not only with an endless supply of serenity and charm, but also with a small studio that Lisa and Mario affectionately refer to as the "Love Shack." Anyone who lives on the water knows that family and friends don't need to be coaxed to come visit. The

OPPOSITE: In the studio living room, an outdoor rug welcomes sandy and salty feet and encourages easy living. Pillows featuring underwater creatures top carefree, slipcovered sofas. "The dresser was left on the curb for trash pick-up," Lisa recalls. "It was solid, but the glossy blue paint was pretty messed up. When Mario began to sand it down to the bare wood we discovered a white layer and decided to stop sanding and keep the distressed look." The hand-carved blue whale from the Philippines has an endearing meaning. "It's believed to have the ability to open people's hearts by simply being in their presence," Lisa recounts.

ABOVE: Bohemian style is all about layering trinkets and treasures to tell a story. Here a voluminous shell holds some of Lisa's starfish collection. These have been dyed to harmonize with the sea glass and the room's oceanic palette. "They remind me of their celestial cousins," Lisa explains. "Sea glass represents all the beautiful coastal colors: the soft blues and greens, and the milky whites."

"Starfish remind me of their celestial cousins, and sea glass represents all the beautiful coastal colors: the soft blues and greens and the milky whites."

PREVIOUS PAGES: Ask Lisa the secret to setting the breezy mood of her chic little beach shack and she will tell you that the biggest impact can be made with the right color, like the variations on a turquoise theme she used in her living room. Though simply furnished with revamped and vintage pieces, the space gets its inviting laid-back mood from its Zen-like quality. Slipcovered sofas, floor pillows, a rattan lantern, and timeworn furnishings herald laid-back bohemian beach living.

OPPOSITE: Another outdoor rug anchors the dining area. The formerly brown table and the old wicker garden chairs were updated and refreshed with a coat of white chalk paint and pillows with a fabric pattern reminiscent of seaweed. Voile curtains allow a view of swaying palm trees outside. Frosted glass containers play dual roles as vases for tropical cuttings or to hold candles after dark.

ABOVE: When your goal is to embrace the boho beach lifestyle, natural accessories like these starfish are the obvious choice.

OVERLEAF: The studio bedroom's pink palette ushers in a cocoon-like tranquil and relaxed spirit, a welcome feeling after a day spent riding waves or just soaking up the hot sun on the beach. When Lisa found the wire pouf at a yard sale it was fluorescent yellow so she spray-painted it to a more suitable pale coral hue. The bed coverlet and one of the surfboards share a rosy backdrop, a floral pattern and a Hawaiian vibe, while the brown surfboard complements the natural wood of the mirror frame. The tall, slender lamp's paper shade introduces a hint of Japanese teahouse style.

LEFT: In the bedroom, the wicker chairs confer an island style to the reading nook. Their deep brown stain recalls the reeds that line the banks of the bay to the rear of the property, while the pillows' coral pattern nods to the waterside location. A garland of starfish dances across the window as yet another sign of the nearby beach.

ABOVE: From the barely-there blush of the shells and flowers to the gentle flush of the pillows, this bedside vignette is dreamy and comforting. Underlying the coastal setting, coral fragments and scallop shells are discreetly displayed in shadow boxes.

OPPOSITE: The "love shack" overlooks the garden and the bay. Lisa set up a hammock to allow guests and their pets to relax, play, and enjoy the peaceful surrounding nature.

Anyone who lives on the water knows that family and friends don't need to be coaxed to come visit. The lure of the beach is their siren's song.

lure of the beach is their siren's song. Even more so when they get to nestle and regroup in a private treehouse-like setting in a lush cove, just steps from the main house.

When decorating the studio, Lisa set out to create a beach-inspired bohemian sanctuary of well-being for her appreciative visitors. "My vision was for anyone to walk in and feel cool and calm, and for the colors to harmonize with the view," she explains. That meant eliminating Old Florida colors like neon yellow and harsh greens. To achieve her desired effect, Lisa opted for a fresh palette that seems selected from the prettiest blues and pinks from a box of Crayola—brilliant blues mirror the waterside location, pinks echo the shells and native flora and fauna, and whites evoke the beach's sugar-like sand.

Relaxed furnishings up the boho factor, while whimsical accents boost the lighthearted vibe, from playfully patterned pillows to collected seashells, sea glass, and other beach-related baubles. By channeling the organic beauty of the little hideaway's location, all objects just seem to belong. The small studio isn't fancy or fussy, but it has an aura of authenticity and friendliness that enchants and radiates with calming energy and soulful beauty.

the CREATIVE BOHEMIAN

In Providence, Rhode Island, the impressive complex known as Rising Sun Mills brings to mind the old saying "Birds of a feather flock together." Built circa 1800 and named after their former function, the textile mills have been revived as live/work studios and lofts for artists and the once-abandoned buildings are now thriving with creatives of all disciplines, including Courtney Webster, an event stylist and project manager for an interior design studio in Boston, and her husband Brandon Aguiar, a painter. "We needed a space that could accommodate Brandon's art studio," Courtney says. "We fell in love with the raw, industrial character of the building with its original large windows, brick walls, and wood floor."

Living in a 1,300-square foot loft with such high ceilings takes some planning design wise. "We struggled a bit with how open the layout is! It was tricky to define spaces without anything feeling closed off," Courtney admits. Yet within the floorplan concept the couple managed to create distinct areas linked by a neutral palette warmed with pink

ABOVE: While global prints are an easy way to message worldly style, textures play an equally important role. When just a small dose is needed, dark wood and a bamboo tray can evoke exotic destinations without going all-out.

OPPOSITE: The sofa, which the couple have had for a few years, received a new slipcover in neutral linen, while a shaggy throw from Urban Outfitters injects a bit of color and a lot of texture. An indigo blue armchair was chosen to provide contrast to the sofa. "We actually sanded the legs to the raw wood—they had been stained an umber color and were too dark," Courtney says. A print from Target marries beautifully with the chair, and mirrors the dining-room wallpaper. The patterned, softly colored rug adds comfort underfoot. The rattan poufs from Ikea are favorites of Courtney—"I love their versatility and material. We can use them at the coffee table or by the swinging chair." As for the shiny gold table, she adds, "We wanted something bold but that would also work well as an end table or a plant stand. We like to juxtapose reflective elements with more rustic ones." Mission accomplished! A ladder adds vertical storage for globally-inspired textiles.

OPPOSITE: "We've always wanted a fun hanging chair for reading and listening to records. This apartment was made for it!" says Courtney, who is also partial to the blanket from Anthropologie and the pillow from Target. "Both have great texture and pattern, but are still neutral. I like that they complement the chair and space." The mirror and bar cart (both from Target) and a nubby and colorful rug from Home Goods contribute to the cozy setting.

LEFT: A vintage bench found on Craigslist and new chairs from Amazon are united with a table made by Courtney's dad and a ceiling fixture from Target. Brandon spray-painted the bench white and Courtney outfitted it with comfy pillows, including a favorite gift from a friend's trip to Vietnam. When entertaining, Courtney likes to set the table with fun and unusual items like the face vase, carved candleholders, wood chargers, and pretty napkins. For the wall separating the main space from the bedroom, Courtney wanted to introduce a bold feature. "We loved the idea of including a large-scale geometric wallpaper and zeroed in on this shibori pattern." To further define the dining room, she opted for a sisal rug from Ikea and a pair of wall sconces. "The room lacks overhead lights, and I like having different lighting options when hosting guests for dinner parties or drinks," she explains. A narrow shelf allows for display possibilities while not competing with the wallpaper pattern. "We recently installed the shelf so these are the original selection of photos, which were taken by me. It's a mix of places we've visited, people we love, and things we've experienced together," Courtney says. "I also love how we can easily change out the photos according to holidays or life events. It offers lots of flexibility!"

PREVIOUS PAGES: The loft's neutral walls and ceiling balance the original wood floor and ground relaxed furnishings in a way that makes the open and airy space look approachable, stylish, and dreamy. By positioning the hanging chair and bar cart between the living and dining-room areas, Courtney and Brandon created a subtle separation between each space without interrupting the visual flow. The décor focuses on light, textures, and a mix of organic and contemporary pieces. "I always love rattan and leather," Courtney says. "They introduce a bohemian vibe and are so versatile." A profusion of plants conveys a greenhouse effect.

"Brandon and I have blended a mix of bohemian, midcentury-modern, and rustic styles in our home to create a true reflection of us."

ABOVE LEFT: The living room is open to the kitchen. Due to rental restrictions, Courtney and Brandon were limited in their update options. However, they were able to add a most personal touch with the richly colored runner on which Courtney walked down the aisle on her wedding day. She also made the best use of the small corner adjacent to the kitchen with a narrow étagère that provides both display areas and concealed storage. The acrylic chair offers additional seating when needed, yet doesn't add bulk thanks to its see-through quality.

ABOVE RIGHT AND OPPOSITE: For her little office, Courtney says she "wanted something minimal that would work well for when I'm blogging or working from home. I love that it has wheels so it's easy to move, as well." She found just the right desk and the companion chair from Wayfair and paired them with a bookshelf from Ikea. The framed print over the desk mimics a window overlooking rooftops. Brandon painted the artwork to the left of the bookshelf.

ABOVE: Courtney's dad attached wood pallets together to form the base for the queen-size bed. A colorful kantha quilt by Kalyana Textiles, a Boston company, adds a vintage touch to the new bed. The neutral macramé wall hanging is just the right decorative touch, while the gold pillow brings a dash of boho glam. A small nightstand and a streamlined side table are all that's needed for books and lamps.

LEFT: Courtney has always had a soft spot for a hippopotamus! "I've just loved hippos forever—I wish I remembered how it started! My family has always gifted me little hippo things since I was a child, so I have a few hippo home décor items, jewelry pieces, and stuffed animals from when I was little."

OPPOSITE: Two paintings set over the small dresser make a definite vintage statement and a sentimental one, too. "They were my grandma's on my dad's side," Courtney explains. "My aunt gifted them to me a few years back. They are painted on tin." A tall Ikea mirror, the frame spray-painted white, adds light and dimension to the small room. "We love how large—and inexpensive—it is!" Courtney exclaims.

and blue color accents. "I love how well they pair with one another and how many different shades of each there are," Courtney notes. Their individual sense of design also comes into play. "Brandon and I have blended a mix of bohemian, midcentury-modern, and rustic styles in our home to create a true reflection of us. We wanted it to feel honest and homey with a mix of functional and stylish pieces," says Courtney, who mines inspiration from design books, Instagram, blogs, and her job. "I'm always surrounded by beautiful fabrics, and am constantly sourcing and selecting items for clients. I get to envision how things would work in my home and love taking that influence and making it my own," she explains.

Courtney describes her style evolution to its present-day contemporary bohemian mood. "It has naturally morphed over the years. In our first apartment together, Brandon and I bought almost strictly Ikea and vintage. Then we started buying almost entirely midcentury modern. That felt too cold, so we introduced different textures and colors and it made the space feel warmer and more inviting. Since then we've only brought in pieces we truly love and it has felt more and more like home."

LEFT: Courtney had wanted a rattan peacock chair for years, so she posted on Facebook to ask if any friends or family members had one. "Someone did have this vintage one and gifted us with it for free!" she recalls. It is now part of a cozy reading nook together with an antique rug, and a modern table and lamp, both from Target.

OPPOSITE: The loft lacks storage and Courtney decided to try the trend known as capsule clothing collections. "It's about limiting yourself to a certain amount of clothing per season," she explains. "I thought it would be nice to try. I then purged a lot of my clothes and keep a curated collection of both Brandon's and mine exposed." A little padded stool lends a spot to sit to put on shoes.

Courtney's rule for mixing fabrics is an easy one to follow. "It's about combining texture, color, and pattern. For example, if you have one large-scale pattern it's always best to pair it with a smaller one. If a pillow or a blanket is super fluffy, offset it with a smooth one. The same is true of color—it's all about balance."

Courtney's advice is to check local thrift stores and also to test out a trend or style at inexpensive stores first. "Don't invest in something until it's tried and true. Love everything you bring into your space and it will never feel out of place." The results speak for themselves: Courtney's and Brandon's home is proof that sophistication and charm on a budget are totally attainable.

the FREE SPIRIT

Gabrielle and Zack Aker lived in two other places prior to moving into their current Los Angeles digs. "We were coming to downtown every weekend to hang out, so we thought why not just move here and then we can walk everywhere!" The couple also wanted the aesthetic of a loft. "When we saw how naturally bright this loft was, we were sold. We could see the potential." Gabrielle recalls. "Some of the other lofts are much darker or they face into the center of the building instead of the street. Zack and I have a very negative reaction to homes that are dark and dingy, but this one was the right one."

Loft living comes with lots of charm but also with some challenges, mostly when it comes to creating a seamlessly warm atmosphere out of an open space with brick walls and concrete floors. But Gabrielle, who is a designer, was ready to tackle any obstacle. "I had worked in other creative fields, but none of them were quite right. I have always had an eye for style and I found my niche in interior design," she says. Her personal taste leans to rustic minimalist with natural elements and cultural influences. "Australian culture has such a laid-back vibe but with a great sense of style. Italian culture is rich in history and beauty. I'd say they appreciate beauty maybe more

OPPOSITE: The loft is a rental and because most of the space is structurally set in place, Zack and Gabrielle had to come up with a décor that would allow their personality to come through. The swing is in answer to their idea of a grown-up playground. Zack built and assembled it, and then secured it to the concrete ceiling with metal hooks. "We knew we wanted a dreamy, childlike, Disneyland feeling," Gabrielle says.

ABOVE: Nestled among greenery and shapely organic driftwood, a bar cart from Urban Outfitters is handy when entertaining, but can also easily be moved to the dining room if needed. A landscape painting found at the Long Beach Antique Market conveys a nostalgic touch to the modern setting.

PREVIOUS PAGES: At 886-square feet, the loft isn't very large, but its ten-foot high ceilings, sleek concrete floor, and five windows, each five feet high, make it appear much more spacious. Gabrielle's design aesthetic includes an abundance of plants and greenery throughout the loft. "It's important to me to bring the outdoors in, especially living in downtown where there is not a lot of green space. I believe that nurturing plants keeps me connected to nature." Gabrielle designed the table and had it made out of poplar wood. "I had been looking for something like this for a while and couldn't find exactly what I had in mind, so I decided to have it made," she says. "The chairs are teakwood and come from Indonesia, as does the wooden bowl. I loved their bohemian and organic feel, and the wood grain is stunning, raw, and natural." Industrial stools and the pendant light impart a vintage touch.

RIGHT: "The library is Zack's baby—it's always been his dream to have a bookstore one day when we're old. He loves classic literature and has a passion for collecting books," Gabrielle explains. "It took him about a month working every day to build and assemble the bookshelf. He then bought and arranged 1,000 books of literature, including first editions of John Steinbeck's *East of Eden* and *The Grapes of Wrath*. The books are arranged based on what he thought looked pretty." The cozy leather sofa is the perfect companion for the library wall, while the bleached tropical-wood side table imparts an exotic touch. The modern solid slate coffee table from West Elm sits on a soft hued and gently faded rug, while a maidenhair fern lends a graceful green touch. A trip to the Italian countryside inspired the strings of lights suspended in the living area, where Gabrielle hung a total of 300 feet of string bulbs. "I wanted a very messy magical feel. It reminds me of outdoor cafes, which always make my heart happy." Zack sketched the black-and-white portrait of famed jazz saxophonist Joe Henderson on the living-room wall, using chalk and charcoal.

than any other culture. Mexican culture is so lively and colorful. And they make the most beautiful pottery! I love seeing products from other countries that are so interesting and unique," she expresses.

Good design, however, doesn't happen overnight, so Gabrielle and Zack took their time cultivating their ideas. "A studio loft is its own design challenge because you are basically working with a giant rectangle and you have to figure out how to maximize the space while instilling some intimacy," Gabrielle explains. "We moved furniture around and played with different layouts before landing on our current configuration." One of the key steps was to position the furniture in a way that separated the spaces without putting up barriers. "For us, it was all about furniture placement," says Gabrielle. "We wanted our

ABOVE: Since the rental agreement for the loft doesn't allow for changing the countertops or the modern cabinetry, the couple made the best of the situation, but Gabrielle says, "It could be a lot worse!" However, she is considering experimenting with contact paper as a temporary backsplash. And she also plans on adding more baskets, driftwood, and pottery, to expand the display on top of the cabinets. "The baskets are practical and hold some kitchen items. I love pottery and want to continue to collect it," she explains.

ABOVE LEFT: The ceiling-hung chair came home from a trip to Tulum, Mexico. It's both a light and comfy addition to the loft, as well as a conversation piece.

ABOVE RIGHT: "I love mixing styles, and this mirror reminds me of Paris. When I fall in love with a piece, I don't care what style it is. I just get it and make it work. The firefly lights are childlike and magical. They make you dream," Gabrielle says.

home to have a magical quality. We love entertaining and making our guests feel like they never want to leave!"

Another element of the couple's aesthetic is less tangible but equally vital. "Zack and I are both very sensitive to the way places feel, so we usually design and redesign based on how we're feeling," Gabrielle explains. "We did select everything together. Zack cares a lot about how our place looks, which is something I actually love. We don't always agree, but he usually defers to me if I really feel that an item he loves won't work in our place since this is what I do for my job." When making decorating decisions, Gabrielle suggests always choosing furnishings that reflect who you are and what you love, rather than just copying what you see on Pinterest and other social media sites. "Don't try to make pieces work when they simply don't fit in your space," she says. "The right furniture will make a home look beautiful, unique, and welcoming."

"Don't try to make pieces work when they simply don't fit your space. The right furniture will make a home look beautiful, unique, and welcoming."

RIGHT: The bedroom's brick wall is a fairly new feature and is an impressive trompe l'oeil. Gabrielle says this space is her favorite area, "probably because of the Rebel brick wallpaper—I am in love with it. We tried a few other designs but this particular one complements the industrial feel of the loft perfectly." She is also very partial to the branch "chandelier" that appears to float above the bed. "I had a vision of how I wanted it to look but couldn't find any pictures, so I decided to make it. I got the branches at Los Angeles Flower Market and configured them, and then Zack and I worked out how to hang it." To add interest to the all-white bedding, Gabrielle chose a throw with interesting texture and a nomadic feel. "We don't have a bedroom door so the bed has to be made every day!" She selected the light pendant for its whimsical flower shape, which plays into her love of nature. To compensate for the lack of closets, she and Zack suspended copper rods from the ceiling to hang clothes.

the FASHIONABLE BOHEMIAN

When I first saw the small guest cottage that came with my house, it was love at first sight. The sun-bleached tin roof and the exposed rafters had an irresistibly seductive bohemian appeal. However, it needed a major decorating face-lift.

I wanted to maintain the integrity of the loft-like feel of the diminutive (450-square feet) home while giving it a fresh, young, and hip look. I planned to enhance the space with colors that would make it appear larger—white was the obvious choice for the walls, ceiling, and beams, but to attain the fashionable look I had in mind, a contrasting color had to be part of the scheme. Painting the floor black, which I did myself using epoxy paint; was the answer. The opposing qualities of the palette maintain a harmonious visual path, while textures and patterns produce a smooth and airy union from one room to the next. The repeated use of both black and white—the former in smaller, but powerful, doses, and the latter in larger and equally impactful ways—provides balance and consistency.

The next challenge was to come up with a way to divide the all-in-one space into specific areas without resorting to physical barriers. Allowing the furnishings to define the "rooms" did the trick.

OPPOSITE: Leather butterfly chairs were chosen over a sofa to create a cozy reading area, rather than an actual living room. With balance in mind, the round ottoman offers a soft counterpoint to their graphic lines.

ABOVE LEFT: While on a shoot, I fell in love with the horseshoe chime in the home being photographed. The gracious homeowner offered it to me. This kind gesture is one of the lovely side effects of my work and one that I will always cherish. The icons bring back memories of a trip to Russia many years ago.

ABOVE RIGHT: The book canvas is a favorite piece I have had for years, and it has moved with me from house to house and room to room. Its height, narrow size, and subject matter harmonize with the peaceful setting.

PREVIOUS PAGES: The white-and-black palette's patterns and textures lend a chic vibe and underscore the modern bohemian spirit of the loft-like space. The aesthetic is rooted in furnishings and objects that make the room feel cultured, not cluttered. In yin-yang fashion, the black wood floors add a masculine touch that balances the more feminine aspects of the décor and provide continuity between the sleeping and living areas.

OPPOSITE: At one end of the main room the roof slopes down and, with two support beams and a floor-to-ceiling window, forms a recessed area that makes a cozy sleeping nook. Continuing the monochromatic palette provides unity, but pillows and bedding give the space its own identity.

ABOVE LEFT: The little black sheep pillow is particularly treasured as it was hand-stitched by my sister. Tasseled pillows emphasize textures, while the striped and scalloped ones add graphic appeal. Their styles, shapes, and patterns work in harmony with the pared-down aesthetic. I wanted to include some art over the bed but it had to be something airy to keep the look uncluttered and I didn't want to spend a lot of money. The answer was to make the heart from chicken wire spray-painted black and weave through a string of little lights.

ABOVE RIGHT: Accessorizing with modern pieces is a good way to keep a space current without taking away from its rustic character. A small Lucite table adds a sleek contemporary vibe yet doesn't interfere with the room's primitive characteristics. The bead-and-heart garland was a gift from a friend in Santa Fe, New Mexico. The little shutters once belonged to an armoire, but I upcycled the two top panels at the small window in place of curtains. Animals big and small are important elements of bohemian design, from both a spiritual and a decorative aspect. Here a canvas depicting an elephant stenciled in gold adds a gentle glow.

The repeated use of both black and white—the former in smaller doses, and the latter in larger and equally impactful ways—provides balance and consistency.

RIGHT: When I was looking for curtains that would make a statement for the floor-to-ceiling window, I came across this panel in Pottery Barn, meant to be used as a faux headboard in a teenager's bedroom. Since it is quite high, I draped it over a rod, creating a double layer and more privacy. It can easily be pushed to one side to allow a view of the garden. A pair of curtains conceals a closet space, doing away with the need for cumbersome doors that would have conflicted with the vintage ones at the entrance to the bathroom. Though it appears to be old, the living-room sideboard is a new piece that I painted gray and whitewashed. The heart candleholders are very dear to me, not only because they were a gift from my sister but also because of their shape.

ABOVE: The claw-foot tub, modern sink, and black accents give the bathroom a spa-like ambience. The vintage medicine cabinet is elevated from its basic function to an artistic presence with a coat of black paint and a lace remnant to conceal its contents.

LEFT: Keeping the look simple but practical meant hiding the washer and dryer behind curtains and making the most of the minimal storage space available. The tall table offers shelves for baskets to corral necessities.

OPPOSITE: A handsome but practical dresser offers room to store clothes, towels, and bed linens, while providing space for plants, candles, and personal items, proving that style and practicality can go hand in hand.

OPPOSITE: When it comes to style, the heft of the reclaimed wood table and the lightness of the acrylic chairs couldn't be more opposing, yet the contrast results in visual harmony as one balances the others. The same principal is applied to the union of the cotton runner with gold placemats and filigree votives. Rather than built-in cabinets, a tall, skinny armoire has been given a new role as a pantry. Trees and plants bring nature in, whimsical animals keep the mood fun and easy, and a profusion of mercury candles romances the room.

ABOVE LEFT: Twinkling lights put the focus on a display of a few favorite photos from past shoots. Blush pink accents from the baskets and flowers add a feminine touch.

ABOVE CENTER: A candelabra, found in Texas, sits on a metal table from France. The mirror creates an illusion of space and light and adds glamour.

ABOVE RIGHT: There is always an underlying romantic theme in my home, whether through hearts, candlelight, objects with a sentimental value, or, in this case, items that speak of affection without saying the words.

Soft touches of blush pinks, warm and glowing brass and gold accents, whimsical art, and plants ushering in fresh green notes, keep the rooms from looking cold and too serious.

Conventional wisdom dictates that in small spaces, the walls should be pale and plain, so that they appear to recede and make a room feel larger. But any free spirit knows that rules don't apply to bohemian décor. In fact, we like to jazz up our walls with eye-catching art and dazzling mirrors for big style statements.

Accessorizing with objects that are light on their feet, have unique shapes, and clean and graphic lines, like glassware, baskets, and wireworks, perpetuates a clutter-free feel and helps establish diverse focal points. Sparkling mercury votives enhance even the most pedestrian finishes, while tactile fabrics promote an organic quality. New and vintage pieces make for an interesting combination. I prefer things not to be too symmetrical so, with a few exceptions (the butterfly chairs being an example), I rarely buy accessories or furniture pieces in pairs.

My guest-house goal was to provide a cozy but chic crash pad for family and guests to escape from life's pressures and rejuvenate in a private environment and, based on their reaction, that's exactly how they feel.

ABOVE: Adjacent to the dining area, the galley-style kitchen keeps pace with the overall black-and-white palette. Though streamlined, it offers all necessary amenities. Open shelving allows easy access to everyday items, while curtains conceal essential storage below.

OPPOSITE TOP LEFT: Drinks always taste better when served in pretty glasses.

OPPOSITE BOTTOM LEFT: An antique candleholder from Italy doubles as a small vase for a posy of violets.

OPPOSITE RIGHT: Moroccan glasses, opalescent bowls from California, and mercury candleholders stand ready for dinner parties.

Pops of color impart festive notes and lively touches to the kitchen, keeping it from looking too serious.

INDEX

ACKNOWLEDGMENTS

Many people have made this book possible starting with the talented team at CICO Books: Cindy Richards, Sally Powell, Gillian Haslam, Anna Galkina, Gurjant Mandair, and Louise Leffler. A very big thank you to each for your help and guidance.

My heartfelt thanks to all the gracious people who welcomed us into their homes and allowed us to intrude in their lives: Gabrielle and Zack Aker, Erin and Creighton Barrett, Sarah and Matt Caliguiri, Lisa and Mario De Pinto, Kristin Joyce and Don Guy, Sharlene and Kevin Kayne, Leslie Nemeth, Kari and John Payne, Kandice and David Ridley, and Courtney Webster and Brandon Aguiar. Your generosity of spirit and your inspiring interiors made our photo shoots easy, fun, and memorable.

Many, many thanks to Mark Lohman for, once again, rising to the challenge and delivering such gorgeous photography. This book wouldn't be what it is without your artistry, professionalism, and dedication.

With much love and appreciation,

Fifi